CRANKS

BREADS & TEACAKES

Compiled by Daphne Swann

Cranks is indebted to Jane Suthering, the well-known home economist. She has worked with Cranks on all its recipe books and has adapted, devised and tested the recipes in this latest series. She was assisted by Louise Pickford.

Pottery for photography kindly loaned by Craftsmen Potters Shop, Marshall Street, London W1.

© Cranks Ltd and Guinness Publishing Ltd 1988
Editor Beatrice Frei
Art editor David Roberts
Illustrations Suzanne Alexander, Edward Bawden and Jane Lydbury
Photographs Grant Symon
Published in Great Britain by Guinness Publishing Ltd,
33 London Road, Enfield, Middlesex, England.

Cranks breads & teacakes.
1. Breads – Recipes
I. Cranks Limited
641.8'15

ISBN 0–85112–381–3

Typeset by Ace Filmsetting Ltd, Frome, Somerset
Printed and bound in Spain by Graficas Reunidas S.A., Madrid

INTRODUCTION

When Cranks opened its first restaurant 27 years ago (in Carnaby Street in London's Soho) its name exactly reflected how most people viewed wholefood and vegetarian restaurants – nutty in more senses than one! Now, of course, the lonely furrow that Cranks then ploughed has become the broad highway for a great many.

From the very beginning Cranks became something of a cult and throughout has remained the benchmark by which all other similar enterprises have to be judged. Not only has there been an unswerving commitment to wholefood and vegetarian food without additives and preservatives (to this day Cranks still uses flour from Pimhill Farm in Shropshire, which was one of the first to become totally organic) but there has also been a vigorous experimentation, innovation and creation of new dishes. And although now the food served at any of Cranks' expanding family of restaurants is sophisticated by comparison with the relatively simple fare of the earliest days, there still remains a satisfying practicality and unfussiness in the recipes which is a refreshing change from the pretentiousness of many restaurants and cookbooks.

The continual creation of new dishes has, over the years, produced a vast number of tried and tested recipes – and it's from this repertoire of new dishes that the very best have been selected for inclusion in this series of books.

NOTES ON INGREDIENTS

Carob The ideal substitute for chocolate. It is made from the ground fruit of the carob tree. Available ground in powder form, in chips or drops, or as a bar which can be grated, melted or simply eaten like chocolate. It is rich in vitamins and contains no refined sugar or caffeine. Available in most health food shops.

Eggs Cranks uses only free-range eggs in its bakeries and, therefore, recommends them in all the recipes. Many free-range eggs are not graded but as a guideline we would use size 3. They are now readily available in most shops – do be sure to look for the label "free-range".

Fat The addition of fat will enrich bread dough and give a moist bread with a soft crust. It also improves the keeping qualities of the bread. Butter, margarine, oils or nutter (a hard white vegetable fat made from nut oils) may be used. Hard fats can be rubbed in to the dry ingredients or melted and added with the liquid.

Flour Cranks uses 100 per cent wholemeal stoneground and organically grown flour in nearly all recipes – thus using the whole of the wheat berry. However, 85 per cent wholemeal flour gives preferable results in some recipes which require a more delicate texture, such as waffles and crumpets. Other flours available include rye, soya, barley, buckwheat, rice, maize and potato. These flours do not make good bread on their own and will need a high proportion of wholewheat flour added to give good results. Rye flour produces a close textured bread with a subtle sour taste; but each of these flours has its own distinctive flavour and texture, providing variety within the finished bread.

Fruit concentrate Apple, pear and other concentrated juices are now available in bottles in most health food stores.

Gluten A protein found in wheat and other grains which strengthens the flour and helps to produce a well risen, good textured loaf. Some people have an intolerance to gluten. We have, therefore, included a few recipes with a very low gluten content. There is minimal or no gluten in oatmeal, millet, buckwheat, potato, barley, rice, maize or soya flours.

Grains and seeds A wide variety of grains and seeds, many of them organically grown and unsprayed, can now be obtained from good health food shops and supermarkets. In this book, we use oatmeal, ryeflakes, rolled oats, bran, millet seed, kibbled wheat (also called cracked wheat), wheatgerm, whole wheat berries and wheat flakes. Also seeds such as sesame, sunflower, caraway, fennel, linseed, coriander, poppy and cumin.

Nutter A pure white vegetable fat made from nut oils – the vegetarian alternative to lard. Sold in cartons in health food shops.

Salt Salt (we use natural sea salt) improves the flavour of bread; however, it should be measured accurately. It prevents the yeast from fermenting too quickly, but too much will arrest the yeast, so it should always be added to the dry ingredients and not to the yeast liquid. In general, 1 tsp (5 ml) salt is required for each 1 lb (450 g) flour.

Sugar Unrefined brown sugar is used in all Cranks recipes. It is free from artificial colourings, and other additives, and is available in various types – demerara, muscovado, light or dark, molasses and golden granulated. Brown sugar lumps and an unrefined caster sugar are also now available. For authenticity, check the packet for the country of origin, usually Mauritius. It is not essential, however, when making yeast dough to add any sweetening agent. It may be left out of the recipe and the yeast frothed successfully with tepid water and a little of the measured flour. This is invaluable for diabetics or those on a sugar-free diet.

Yeast This is available both fresh and dried. Fresh yeast is rather like putty in both colour and texture and crumbles easily when fresh. It may be stored in the refrigerator for up to 1 month and will freeze for up to 6 months, although it becomes very creamy in consistency when thawed. Always ensure that it is well wrapped in cling film or kitchen foil for storage. There are two types of dried yeast, granular and easy blend, which is almost like powder and can be added straight to the flour. Follow packet directions when using either type.

When using fresh or dried (granular) yeast, it should be mixed with tepid liquid (98.4°F/36.9°C) and left in a warm place to froth for 10–15 minutes to activate it prior to adding to the flour. A little sugar is usually added to the yeast liquid to encourage frothing but too much will stop the yeast working. The proportion of yeast used in a recipe is dependent on the ingredients. Enriched doughs need a higher proportion of yeast than plain breads because its growth is retarded by additional fat, sugar, eggs and fruit. Half the quantity of dried yeast is required to fresh yeast. ½ oz (15 g) dried yeast is equivalent to 1 oz (25 g) fresh yeast.

HINTS ON BREAD MAKING

KNEADING

The Cranks Wholemeal Loaf which was based on the Grant Loaf (developed by Doris Grant in the 1950s) eliminates both kneading and second proving; the resulting dough makes an excellent loaf and is quick and easy to prepare.

Traditionally, however, kneading is one of the most important stages of bread making because it develops the gluten (see p. 9) which gives dough its elasticity and distributes the yeast so that the dough rises evenly. In general, 8–10 minutes kneading is suggested. If available, use the dough hook attachment of an electric mixer, or a food processor. Alternatively, knead by hand.

To knead by hand: place the dough on a lightly floured surface and form a neat ball. Push the dough down and away from the body with the palms of both hands, then fold back towards the centre with the fingertips. Give the dough a quarter turn and repeat the process in a continuous movement.

The dough is ready when it is no longer sticky, is smooth, elastic and firm.

LIQUID

The amount of liquid used in a recipe will vary according to the absorbency of the flour and dry ingredients. Too much liquid gives a spongy open texture.

Water is the most usual liquid for plain breads. Milk or fruit juices may also be used.

Milk adds extra food value, helps to strengthen the dough and improves the keeping qualities of the bread.

In general, ½ pt (300 ml) liquid is required for each 1 lb (450 g) of flour.

SHAPING THE DOUGH FOR THE TIN

Knead the dough quickly then punch down to flatten and remove air bubbles. Fold in the sides and roll up firmly. Place seam side down in an oiled tin.

SHAPING FREE FORM LOAVES OR ROLLS

Knead the dough into a smooth ball and, using a sharp knife, cut slashes in the top of the dough. Place on an oiled baking tray.

SOME ALTERNATIVE WAYS OF SHAPING THE DOUGH

LOAVES

Cottage loaf Cut off about one quarter of the dough. Shape the large portion into a neat ball and make a big hole through the centre. Shape the small portion into a pear shape and place pointed side down on to the hole.

Log loaf Knead the dough quickly, then punch down to flatten and remove air bubbles. Roll up to a log shape and pinch the ends together. Place seam side down and using a sharp knife, cut slashes in the top of the dough.

Plait Shape the dough into three equal batons. Lay the batons side by side. Pinch one end together and then plait the batons together. Pinch the opposite end to secure.

Twist Shape the dough into two equal batons and lay them side by side. Pinch one end together and twist one baton carefully around the other. Pinch the opposite end to secure.

ROLLS

Crescents Roll the dough to a large round 8–10 in (20–25 cm) diameter. Divide into wedges, then roll each wedge, starting at the wide end. Curve the ends round to form crescents.

Tiered rolls Roll out the dough to a rectangle about ⅛th in (3 mm) thick. Brush with melted butter and cut into strips 2–3 in (5–7.5 cm) wide. Sprinkle with seeds of your choice if wished. Stack six strips together and cut into squares.

Flower rolls Shape small pieces of dough into balls and flatten slightly. Snip six evenly spaced cuts in the edge of each roll.

Knots Roll each piece of dough to a baton about 8 in (20 cm) long. Tie each one in a knot.

Round rolls Shape small pieces of dough into balls. Place well apart on oiled baking trays. For a batch of rolls, place the balls of dough just touching on a baking tray.

Torpedo rolls Shape small pieces of dough into ovals, tapering at each end. Make a deep slash lengthways in each one.

RISING OR PROVING

Yeast doughs must be allowed to rise at least once before baking. For many recipes, Cranks only rises the dough once it is shaped for baking. Cover the shaped dough with oiled polythene and leave in a warm place until doubled in size, or until the dough reaches the top of the tin.

If time allows, the dough may be proved after the initial kneading. Place the dough in a lightly oiled bowl. Cover with oiled polythene and leave in a warm place until doubled in size.

In general, rising will take about 45 minutes to 1 hour in a warm place, but the dough may be left in a cool place for 8–12 hours or in the refrigerator for about 24 hours. Slow rising is supposed to give the best, most even results.

GLAZING

To give a crusty finish to bread and rolls, brush the shaped and risen dough with salt or sugar glaze (see p. 92) before baking. For a softer crust, brush with oil or egg glaze (see p. 92). To give baked breads and buns a shiny finish brush them, straight from the oven, with honey or fruit concentrate such as apple or pear. Melted butter may also be used as a glaze on baked goods.

TOPPINGS

Grain flakes, such as rye, oats or barley, kibbled (cracked) wheat, and many seeds, such as sesame, sunflower, poppy, aniseed, caraway and fennel may be sprinkled over shaped doughs before baking.

After baking, sticky glazed sweet doughs may be sprinkled with seeds or chopped nuts.

BAKING

Bread is baked at a high temperature to arrest the action of the yeast so that the dough does not continue to rise. In general, plain breads are baked between 425–450°F/220–230°C/gas mark 7–8. The richer breads are usually baked at a slightly lower temperature as they tend to brown more easily. Suggested temperatures are usually 375–400°F/190–200°C/gas mark 5–6. If breads are browning too quickly, cover with kitchen foil during cooking.

When cooked, bread should sound hollow when tapped on the base and sides. For a firm, crisp crust, cool breads on a wire tray.

STORING AND FREEZING

Fresh bread should be well cooled before storing in an airtight tin or polythene bag in a cool place, and generally it will keep for 1–2 weeks.

Most breads freeze well for up to 2 months, although the crust tends to lift quickly on highly baked breads.

Leave breads to thaw in the sealed polythene bag to prevent drying out. Crisp the crust by placing in a hot oven for about 10 minutes. Many sweet breads are best warmed gently before serving.

All the recipes in this book will freeze.

BREADS & TEACAKES

*B*read has been termed "the staff of life" and it has always played a central part in Western diets.

Nowadays, a great variety of breads are to be found in our shops but there still is nothing quite like the aroma and taste of freshly made bread at home. The satisfaction of making it successfully is exciting and rewarding and it is delicious to eat!

Most recipes in this book are based on the use of yeasted dough made with wholemeal flour. You will be surprised at the many different ways in which it can be used. Once you have mastered the art – and it's not difficult – you will never want commercial bread again! Start off with the Cranks "no-kneading" Wholemeal Loaf – easy and quick to make – and from there all the rest will follow!

CRANKS WHOLEMEAL BREAD

This is the original recipe based on Doris Grant's loaf. It is still made today in Cranks' bakeries, using organically-grown stone-ground flour from Pimhill Farm in Shropshire, where organic farming was pioneered over 40 years ago.

Wholemeal flour 3 lb (1.35 kg)
Salt 1 tbsp (15 ml)
Fresh yeast 1 oz (25 g)
Unrefined brown sugar 1 tbsp (15 ml)
Water, tepid 1½ pts (900 ml)

Mix the flour and salt in a bowl. Mix the yeast, sugar and half the water and leave in a warm place until frothy – about 10 minutes.

Pour the yeast liquid into the flour with the remaining water and mix to give a soft dough.

Place the dough on a lightly-floured surface, divide and shape into two equal portions and transfer to two oiled 2 lb (900 g) loaf tins. Cover with oiled polythene and leave in a warm place until doubled in size – about 1 hour. Bake at 425°F/220°C/gas mark 7 for 35–40 minutes. Cool on a wire tray.

Makes 2 loaves

For baps, roll out the dough thickly on a lightly-floured surface and stamp out eighteen 4 in (10 cm) rounds. Place on a lightly-oiled baking tray. Cover and leave to rise in a warm place until doubled in size – 30–45 minutes. Brush lightly with milk and bake at 400°F/200°C/gas mark 6 for 20–25 minutes. Cool on a wire tray.

For rolls, see also "Some alternative ways of shaping the dough", p. 13.

MALT 'N' BROWN LOAVES

The malted flour gives a special flavour to this bread.

Malted wholewheat flour 3 lb (1.35 kg)
Salt 1 tbsp (15 ml)
Fresh yeast ¾ oz (20 g)
Water, tepid 1½ pt (900 ml)
Malt extract 1 tbsp (15 ml)
Oil to glaze
Sugar glaze (see p. 92)

Combine the flour and salt in a large bowl.

Mix the yeast with half the water and add to the flour with the malt extract, then gradually add the rest of the water and mix to a soft dough. Knead for 8–10 minutes.

Divide the mixture into five portions.

Knead one portion and place in an oiled 1 lb (450 g) loaf tin, knead two portions together and place in an oiled 2 lb (900 g) loaf tin. Repeat with the last two portions.

Cover with oiled polythene and leave in a warm place for 45 minutes to 1 hour until doubled in size. Brush lightly with oil and then with sugar glaze.

Bake at 425°F/220°C/gas mark 7 for 25–40 minutes, depending on the size. Cool on a wire tray.

Makes 2 large loaves and 1 small one

RYE BREAD

Wholemeal flour 1 lb (450 g)
Rye flour 6 oz (175 g)
Salt 1½ tsp (7.5 ml)
Caraway seeds 1½ tsp (7.5 ml)
Butter or nutter 2 oz (50 g)
Fresh yeast ¾ oz (20 g)
Unrefined brown sugar 1 tbsp (15 ml)
Water, tepid ⅔ pt (400 ml)
Sugar glaze (see p. 92)

Combine the flours, salt and 1 tsp (5 ml) of the caraway seeds in a large bowl, and rub in the butter.

Mix the yeast, sugar and half the water and leave in a warm place for about 10 minutes until frothy.

Add the yeast liquid to the dry ingredients with the remaining water and knead for 8–10 minutes.

On a lightly-floured surface shape the dough into a round. Place on an oiled baking tray. Cover with oiled polythene and leave in a warm place until doubled in size – 30–45 minutes. Brush with sugar glaze and sprinkle with the remaining caraway seeds. Make three slashes on the surface.

Bake at 425°F/220°C/gas mark 7 for about 40 minutes. Cool on a wire tray.

Makes 1 loaf

SOYA BREAD

The addition of soya flour to this bread increases the protein content.

Wholemeal flour 14 oz (400 g)
Soya flour 2 oz (50 g)
Salt 1 tsp (5 ml)
Fresh yeast ½ oz (15 g)
Unrefined brown sugar 1 tsp (5 ml)
Water, tepid ½ pt (300 ml)

Combine the flours and salt in a bowl. Mix the yeast, sugar and half the water together and leave in a warm place for about 10 minutes, until frothy.

Add the yeast liquid to the dry ingredients with the remaining water and mix to a soft dough. Knead for 8–10 minutes, then shape into an oval on a lightly-floured surface.

Place on an oiled baking tray, cover with oiled polythene and leave in a warm place until doubled in size – 20–30 minutes.

Bake at 425°F/220°C/gas mark 7 for about 35 minutes. Cool on a wire tray.

Makes 1 loaf

BRAN PLUS LOAF

Cranks introduced this loaf in the 1960s in response to the need for added fibre in the diet.

Wholemeal flour 1 lb (450 g)
Bran 3 oz (75 g)
Salt 1 tsp (5 ml)
Butter or nutter 1 oz (25 g)
Fresh yeast ½ oz (15 g)
Unrefined brown sugar 1 tbsp (15 ml)
Water, tepid ¾ pt (450 ml)
Oil to glaze
Bran to sprinkle

Combine the flour, bran and salt in a large bowl, and rub in the butter. Mix the yeast, sugar and half the water and leave in a warm place for about 10 minutes until frothy.

Add the yeast liquid to the dry ingredients with the remaining water and mix to a soft dough. Knead for 8–10 minutes, shape on a lightly-floured surface then transfer to an oiled 2 lb (900 g) loaf tin. Brush with oil and sprinkle with a little bran.

Cover with oiled polythene and leave in a warm place for 45 minutes to 1 hour until doubled in size.

Bake at 425°F/220°C/gas mark 7 for about 40 minutes. Cool on a wire tray.

Makes 1 loaf

BREWERY BREAD

Dedicated to Guinness, our Publishers!

Fresh yeast ½ oz (15 g)
Honey 1 tbsp (15 ml)
Water 9 tbsp (135 ml)
Rye flour 8 oz (225 g)
Wholemeal flour 8 oz (225 g)
Salt 1 tsp (5 ml)
Guinness ¼ pt (150 ml)

Mix the yeast with the honey and 4 tbsp (60 ml) tepid water. Leave in a warm place for about 10 minutes until frothy.

Combine the flours and salt in a large bowl.

Add 5 tbsp (75 ml) boiling water to the Guinness and add this to the flour with the yeast liquid. Mix to a soft dough then knead for 8–10 minutes.

Place in an oiled bowl, cover with oiled polythene and leave in a warm place until doubled in size – about 1 hour.

On a lightly-floured surface, knead the dough quickly, then shape into a neat round. Place on an oiled baking tray. Cover with oiled polythene and leave to rise until doubled in size – about 45 minutes.

Bake at 425°F/220°C/gas mark 7 for 35–40 minutes. Cool on a wire tray.

Makes 1 loaf

BLACK BREAD

Not exactly black but a very rich dark brown bread.
Serve with cheese and pickles.

Fresh yeast ½ oz (15 g)
Water, tepid 9 fl oz (275 ml)
Unrefined brown sugar 1 tbsp (15 ml)
Rye flour 8 oz (225 g)
Wholemeal flour 8 oz (225 g)
Carob powder 2 tbsp (30 ml)
Salt 1 tsp (5 ml)
Oil 2 tbsp (30 ml)

Mix the yeast, water and sugar and leave in a warm
place for about 10 minutes until frothy.

Combine the flours, carob powder and salt in a
large bowl. Add the oil and yeast liquid and mix to a
soft dough. Knead for 8–10 minutes.

Divide the mixture in half. On a lightly-floured
surface, knead each portion quickly. Transfer to two
oiled 1 lb (450 g) loaf tins.

Cover with oiled polythene and leave in a warm
place for about 45 minutes until doubled in size.

Bake at 425°F/220°C/gas mark 7 for about 25
minutes. Cool on a wire tray.

Makes 2 loaves

WHOLEWHEAT HONEY COB

Fresh yeast 1 oz (25 g)
Water, tepid ½ pt (300 ml)
Salt 1 tsp (5 ml)
Honey 3 tbsp (45 ml)
Oil 1 tbsp (15 ml)
Wholemeal flour 1 lb (450 g)
Wholewheat grains 2 oz (50 g)
Kibbled wheat or wholemeal flour to sprinkle

Mix together the fresh yeast, half the water, salt, honey and oil. Stir in half the flour, beat well, cover and leave in a warm place for 30 minutes.

Stir in the remaining flour and the wholewheat grains with the remaining water and knead for 8–10 minutes to give a smooth elastic dough. Place in a large oiled bowl. Cover with oiled polythene and leave in a warm place until doubled in size – about 30 minutes.

Knead the dough quickly on a lightly-floured surface and shape into a neat round.

Place on an oiled baking tray, cut a deep cross in the top. Brush with water and sprinkle with a little kibbled wheat or flour. Cover loosely and leave in a warm place for 15 minutes.

Bake at 425°F/220°C/gas mark 7 for 40–45 minutes. Cool on a wire tray.

Makes 1 loaf

WHEAT 'N' RYE BREAD

Wholemeal flour 2 lb (900 g)
Rye flour 6 oz (175 g)
Wheat flakes 4 oz (100 g)
Salt 1 tbsp (15 ml)
Fresh yeast ¾ oz (20 g)
Water, tepid 1¼ pt (750 ml)
Molasses 1 tbsp (15 ml)
Wheat flakes to sprinkle

Combine the flours with the wheat flakes and salt in a large bowl. Mix the yeast with half the water and add to the dry ingredients with the molasses and remaining water. Mix to form a smooth dough. Knead for 8–10 minutes.

Transfer the dough to a lightly-floured surface and divide into two portions. Place into two lightly-oiled 2 lb (900 g) loaf tins. Cover with oiled polythene and leave in a warm place until doubled in size – about 1 hour.

Brush with water and sprinkle with wheatflakes. Bake at 425°F/220°C/gas mark 7 for about 40 minutes. Cool on a wire tray.

Makes 2 loaves

SUNFLOWER & HONEY BREAD

Wholemeal flour 3 lb (1.35 kg)
Salt 1 tbsp (15 ml)
Sunflower seeds 3 oz (75 g)
Fresh yeast ¾ oz (20 g)
Water, tepid 1½ pt (900 ml)
Honey 1 tbsp (15 ml)

Combine the flour, salt and sunflower seeds in a large bowl. Mix the yeast with half the water and add to the flour with the honey and remaining water and mix to form a smooth dough. Knead for 10 minutes. Transfer to a lightly-floured surface and divide into five equal portions. Shape each portion and place in a lightly-oiled 1 lb (450 g) loaf tin. Cover with oiled polythene and leave in a warm place until doubled in size – about 45 minutes.

Bake at 425°F/220°C/gas mark 7 for 25–30 minutes. Cool on a wire tray.

Makes 5 loaves

ENRICHED MILK BREAD

Fresh yeast 1 oz (25 g)
Unrefined brown sugar 1 tsp (5 ml)
Milk, tepid 8 fl oz (250 ml)
Wholemeal flour 1 lb (450 g)
Salt ½ tsp (2.5 ml)
Butter, melted 1 oz (25 g)
Free-range egg, beaten 1

Mix the yeast, sugar and milk and leave in a warm place for about 10 minutes until frothy.

Combine the flour and salt. Add the yeast liquid, butter and egg and mix to a soft dough. Knead for 8–10 minutes.

Transfer to a lightly-floured surface and shape into an oblong. Place in an oiled 2 lb (900 g) loaf tin.

Cover with oiled polythene and leave in a warm place until doubled in size – about 45 minutes.

Bake at 425°F/220°C/gas mark 7 for about 40 minutes. Cool on a wire tray.

Makes 1 loaf

PUMPERNICKEL

A traditional, close-textured rye bread favoured in Eastern Europe – ideal for open sandwiches.

Rye flour 1 lb (450 g)
Salt 1 tsp (5 ml)
Water, tepid ½ pt (300 ml)
Molasses 2 tbsp (30 ml)

Combine the flour and salt in a bowl. Mix the molasses with the water and add to the flour. Mix thoroughly to form a smooth dough. Transfer the dough to a well buttered 1½ pt (900 ml) pudding basin. Cover with kitchen foil.

Place the pudding basin in a saucepan of simmering water. Cover and steam for 3 hours. Refill the pan as necessary. Turn out and cool on a wire tray.

Makes 1 loaf

OATMEAL & TREACLE BREAD

Wholemeal flour 3 lb (1.35 kg)
Salt 1 tbsp (15 ml)
Rolled oats 6 oz (175 g)
Fresh yeast 1 oz (25 g)
Unrefined brown sugar 1 tsp (5 ml)
Water, tepid 4 tbsp (60 ml)
Milk 1½ pt (900 ml)
Butter 2 oz (50 g)
Black treacle 4 tbsp (60 ml)
Milk to glaze
Rolled oats to sprinkle

Mix together the flour, salt and oats in a large bowl.
Combine the yeast, sugar and water and leave in a
warm place until frothy – about 10 minutes.

Put the milk, butter and black treacle into a
saucepan and heat gently until the butter has melted.
Cool until tepid.

Pour the yeast liquid and milk mixture into the dry
ingredients, mix well, then knead for 8–10 minutes.
Place the dough on a lightly-floured surface and
divide into two portions. Knead quickly, then transfer
to two oiled 2 lb (900 g) loaf tins. Cover with oiled
polythene and leave until doubled in size – about 1
hour.

Brush with milk and sprinkle with oats. Bake at
425°F/220°C/gas mark 7 for 35–40 minutes. Cool on
a wire tray.

Makes 2 loaves

KIBBLED WHEAT COBS

Wholemeal flour 1 lb (450 g)
Rye flour 2 oz (50 g)
Kibbled wheat 4 oz (100 g)
Salt 1 tsp (5 ml)
Fresh yeast ½ oz (15 g)
Unrefined brown sugar 1 tsp (5 ml)
Water, tepid 12 fl oz (350 ml)
Black treacle 1 oz (25 g)
Salt glaze (see p. 92)
Kibbled wheat to sprinkle

Combine the flours, kibbled wheat and salt in a large bowl. Mix together the yeast, sugar and half the water and leave in a warm place until frothy – about 10 minutes. Mix the yeast liquid with the dry ingredients together with the treacle and remaining water. Knead for 8–10 minutes. Place the dough on a lightly-floured surface, cut in half and shape into two rounds.

Place on lightly-oiled baking trays, cover with oiled polythene and leave in a warm place until doubled in size – 20–30 minutes.

Brush with salt glaze and sprinkle with kibbled wheat and bake at 425°F/220°C/gas mark 7 for about 30 minutes. Cool on a wire tray.

Makes 2 loaves

RICE BREAD

Water 18 fl oz (550 ml)
Brown rice 3 oz (75 g)
Salt 2 tsp (10 ml)
Wholemeal flour 1 lb (450 g)
Fresh yeast ½ oz (15 g)
Unrefined brown sugar 1 tsp (5 ml)

Bring 12 fl oz (350 ml) water to the boil in a saucepan. Add the rice and half the salt and cook, covered, for 25 minutes. Remove the lid and cook rapidly, stirring, until all the water is absorbed.

Mix the flour and remaining salt in a large bowl.

Warm the remaining water till tepid and mix in the yeast and sugar. Leave in a warm place for about 10 minutes until frothy, then add to the flour with the rice. Mix to a soft dough, then knead for 8–10 minutes.

Place the dough in an oiled bowl, cover with oiled polythene and leave in a warm place for about 1 hour until doubled in size.

On a lightly-floured surface, knead the dough quickly, then transfer to an oiled 2 lb (900 g) loaf tin. Cover with oiled polythene and leave to rise in a warm place until doubled in size – about 1 hour.

Bake at 425°F/220°C/gas mark 7 for 35–40 minutes. Cool on a wire tray.

Makes 1 loaf

FRENCH WALNUT BREAD

Fresh yeast ½ oz (15 g)
Honey 1 tbsp (15 ml)
Water, tepid ½ pt (300 ml)
Walnuts, chopped 3 oz (75 g)
Walnut oil 2 tbsp (30 ml)
Wholemeal flour 1 lb (450 g)
Salt 1 tsp (5 ml)
Sugar glaze (see p. 92)

Combine the yeast, honey and water and leave in a warm place for about 10 minutes until frothy.

Roast 2½ oz (65 g) of the walnuts at 350°F/180°C/ gas mark 4 for about 10 minutes until golden.

Combine the flour, salt and toasted walnuts in a large bowl. Add the walnut oil and yeast liquid and mix to a soft dough.

Knead for 8–10 minutes, then place in an oiled bowl, cover with oiled polythene and leave in a warm place for about 1 hour until doubled in size.

On a lightly-floured surface, knead the dough quickly and transfer to an oiled 2 lb (900 g) loaf tin.

Cover with oiled polythene and leave in a warm place to rise until doubled in size – about 1 hour. Brush with sugar glaze and sprinkle with the remaining walnuts. Bake at 425°F/220°C/gas mark 7 for 35–40 minutes. Cool on a wire tray.

Makes 1 loaf

MULTI-SEED BREAD

A most nutritious bread with a delicious flavour.

Kibbled wheat 2 tbsp (30 ml)
Millet seeds 2 tbsp (30 ml)
Water 12 fl oz (350 ml)
Molasses 1 tbsp (15 ml)
Oil 2 tbsp (30 ml)
Fresh yeast ¾ oz (20 g)
Wheat germ 2 tbsp (30 ml)
Sunflower seeds 2 tbsp (30 ml)
Sesame seeds 2 tbsp (30 ml)
Linseed 1 tbsp (15 ml)
Wholemeal flour 1 lb (450 g)
Salt 1 tsp (5 ml)

Place the kibbled wheat and millet seed in a saucepan with half the water and bring to the boil. Remove from the heat and add the molasses, oil and remaining water. If necessary, allow to cool until tepid, then add the yeast and leave in a warm place until frothy – about 10 minutes.

Place the remaining ingredients in a large bowl, add the yeast liquid and mix to a soft dough.

Knead the dough for 8–10 minutes. Transfer to an oiled bowl and cover with oiled polythene. Leave in a warm place to rise for about 1 hour until doubled in size.

On a lightly-floured surface knead the dough quickly, then transfer to an oiled 2 lb (900 g) loaf tin.

Cover with oiled polythene and leave in a warm place until doubled in size – about 1 hour.

Bake at 425°F/220°C/gas mark 7 for 35–40 minutes.

Cool on a wire tray.

Makes 1 loaf

SPOON BREAD

American Corn Bread which was originally baked in a dish and spooned out.

Wholemeal flour 12 oz (350 g)
Cornmeal (maize flour) 8 oz (225 g)
Salt 1 tsp (5 ml)
Fresh yeast ½ oz (15 g)
Clear honey 2 tbsp (30 ml)
Water, tepid 8 fl oz (250 ml)
Milk, tepid 8 fl oz (250 ml)
Oil 1 tbsp (15 ml)
Free-range egg, beaten 1

Mix the flours and salt together in a large bowl. Mix the yeast, honey and water together and leave until frothy – about 10 minutes.

Add the yeast liquid, milk, oil and egg to the dry ingredients. Beat well, cover and leave in a warm place for 30 minutes. Stir the mixture thoroughly and transfer to an oiled 2 lb (900 g) loaf tin. Cover and leave to prove for a further 20 minutes.

Bake at 400°F/200°C/gas mark 6 for 35–40 minutes. Cool on a wire tray.

Makes 1 loaf

POTATO SODA BREAD

The addition of potato keeps this bread moist and
fresh.

Wholemeal self-raising flour 1 lb (450 g)
Bicarbonate of soda 1 tsp (5 ml)
Salt 1 tsp (5 ml)
Butter 1 oz (25 g)
Potato, cooked and sieved 8 oz (225 g)
Free-range egg, beaten 1
Buttermilk, milk or soya milk ½ pt (300 ml)

Combine the dry ingredients in a bowl and rub in the
butter. Add the potato and mix to a soft dough with
the egg and buttermilk.

Knead quickly on a lightly-floured surface and
shape into an 8 in (20 cm) round.

Place on a buttered baking tray and cut a cross in
the centre. Bake at 400°F/200°C/gas mark 6 for 40–45
minutes. Cool on a wire tray.

Variation
Brush the top of the shaped dough with buttermilk or
milk and sprinkle with seeds such as fennel, celery or
dill before baking.

Makes 1 loaf

PUMPKIN BREAD

Pumpkin purée replaces most of the liquid in this recipe. This results in a flavoursome, moist loaf.

Pumpkin, peeled, seeds removed and chopped
12 oz (350 g)
Butter 1 oz (25 g)
Small onion, finely chopped 1
Fresh yeast ½ oz (15 g)
Unrefined brown sugar 1 tsp (5 ml)
Wholemeal flour 1 lb (450 g)
Salt 1 tsp (5 ml)
Egg glaze (see p. 92)

Steam the pumpkin for 10–15 minutes until tender. Drain and reserve 2 fl oz (50 ml) of the cooking liquid. Purée the pumpkin in a liquidizer.

Melt the butter and sauté the onion until transparent.

Mix the yeast, reserved cooking liquid and sugar together and leave in a warm place for about 10 minutes until frothy.

Combine the flour and salt. Add the yeast liquid, pumpkin purée and onion and mix to a soft dough. Knead for 8–10 minutes, then transfer to a lightly-floured surface. Cut off a small piece of dough (about 1 oz/25 g).

Shape the remaining dough into a neat round and place on an oiled baking tray. Shape the small portion of dough into a 2 in (5 cm) baton and press on to the centre of the round.

Cover with oiled polythene and leave in a warm place until doubled in size – about 45 minutes.

With a sharp knife, make cuts in the dough all the way round to resemble a pumpkin.

Brush the dough with egg glaze and bake at 425°F/220°C/gas mark 7 for 35–40 minutes. Cool on a wire tray.

Makes 1 loaf

FRESH GINGER, CORIANDER & ORANGE BREAD

Fresh yeast ½ oz (15 g)
Honey 1 tbsp (15 ml)
Water, tepid 3 fl oz (75 ml)
Wholemeal flour 1 lb (450 g)
Salt 1 tsp (5 ml)
Ground coriander 2 tsp (10 ml)
Root ginger, finely grated 1 tbsp (15 ml)
Natural yoghourt ¼ pt (150 ml)
Water, boiling 4 tbsp (60 ml)
Orange, finely grated rind of 1

Mix the yeast, honey and water together and leave in a warm place for about 10 minutes until frothy.

In a large bowl, mix the flour, salt, coriander and grated ginger.

Mix the natural yoghourt with the boiling water and orange rind and add to the dry ingredients with the yeast liquid. Mix to a soft dough then knead for 8–10 minutes.

Place in an oiled bowl and cover with oiled polythene. Leave in a warm place until doubled in size – about 1 hour.

On a lightly-floured surface, knead the dough quickly, then transfer to an oiled 2 lb (900 g) loaf tin.

Cover with oiled polythene and leave to rise until doubled in size – about 1 hour. Bake at 425°F/220°C/gas mark 7 for 35–40 minutes. Cool on a wire tray.

Makes 1 loaf

GARLIC & HERB STICKS

Fresh yeast ½ oz (15 g)
Unrefined brown sugar 1 tsp (5 ml)
Water, tepid ½ pt (300 ml)
Wholemeal flour 1 lb (450 g)
Salt 1½ tsp (7.5 ml)
Garlic cloves, crushed 2–4
Black pepper, coarsely ground 1 tsp (5 ml)
Assorted fresh herbs, such as parsley, thyme, basil, sage,
marjoram or rosemary, finely chopped 6 tbsp (90 ml)
Egg glaze (see p. 92)

Mix together the yeast, sugar and water and leave in a
warm place for about 10 minutes until frothy.

Combine the remaining ingredients in a large bowl.
Add the yeast liquid and mix to a soft dough. Knead
for 8–10 minutes until elastic and no longer sticky.

Place in a lightly-oiled bowl, cover with oiled
polythene and leave in a warm place until doubled in
size – about 1 hour.

On a lightly-floured surface, knead the dough
quickly, divide in half and shape each piece into a
French stick about 12 in (30 cm) long. Mark slashes
along the length of each one.

Place on lightly-oiled baking trays, cover with oiled
polythene and leave in a warm place until doubled in
size – 30–45 minutes. Brush with egg glaze.

Bake at 425°F/220°C/gas mark 7 for 20 minutes.
Cool on a wire tray.

Makes 2 sticks

APRICOT & NUT LOAF

This is not a sweetened bread so may be served with soups and savouries.

Fresh yeast ½ oz (15 g)
Honey 1 tbsp (15 ml)
Water, tepid ¼ pt (150 ml)
Wholemeal flour 1 lb (450 g)
Salt 1 tsp (5 ml)
Dried apricots, diced 4 oz (100 g)
Whole almonds, toasted and chopped 2 oz (50 g)
Orange juice ¼ pt (150 ml)

Mix the yeast, honey and water and leave in a warm place for about 10 minutes until frothy.

Place the remaining ingredients in a large bowl. Add the yeast liquid and mix to a soft dough.

Knead for 8–10 minutes. Place in an oiled bowl, cover with oiled polythene and leave in a warm place for about 1 hour until doubled in size. On a lightly-floured surface, knead the dough quickly and then transfer to an oiled 2 lb (900 g) loaf tin. Cover with oiled polythene and leave in a warm place for about 1 hour until doubled in size.

Bake at 425°F/220°C/gas mark 7 for 35–40 minutes. Cool on a wire tray.

Variation
Date & Walnut: Replace apricots with dates and almonds with walnuts.

Makes 1 loaf

SAVOURY APPLE BREAD

Dried apple rings, finely chopped 2 oz (50 g)
Apple juice ½ pt (300 ml)
Dried sage 2 tsp (10 ml)
Fresh yeast ½ oz (15 g)
Unrefined brown sugar 1 tsp (5 ml)
Water, tepid 4 tbsp (60 ml)
Wholemeal flour 1 lb (450 g)
Salt 1½ tsp (7.5 ml)
Apple concentrate to glaze

Place the diced apple, apple juice and dried sage in a saucepan. Bring just to the boil, then remove from the heat and leave to cool.

Mix the yeast, sugar and water and leave in a warm place for about 10 minutes until frothy.

Combine the flour and salt in a large bowl. Add the yeast liquid and the apple pieces with their juice. Mix to a soft dough, then knead for 8–10 minutes.

Place in an oiled bowl and cover with oiled polythene and leave in a warm place for about 1 hour until doubled in size.

On a lightly-floured surface, knead the dough quickly and transfer to an oiled 2 lb (900 g) loaf tin. Cover with oiled polythene and leave for about 1 hour until doubled in size.

Bake at 425°F/220°C/gas mark 7 for 35–40 minutes. Cool on a wire tray. Brush the surface of the loaf with apple concentrate.

Makes 1 loaf

BANANA & COCONUT LOAF

Serve this with spicy vegetable stews.

Large bananas, mashed 2
Water, boiling, about ¼ pt (150 ml)
Fresh yeast ½ oz (15 g)
Honey 1 tbsp (15 ml)
Wholemeal flour 1 lb (450 g)
Salt 1 tsp (5 ml)
Shredded coconut 2 oz (50 g)

Place the mashed banana in a measuring jug and make up to ½ pt (300 ml) with the boiling water.

There should be 3–4 tablespoons of water left. Allow this to cool, then add the yeast and honey. Leave in a warm place until frothy – about 10 minutes.

Mix the flour, salt and coconut in a large bowl. Add the banana mixture and the yeast liquid; mix to a soft dough. Knead for 8–10 minutes.

Place in an oiled bowl, cover with oiled polythene and leave in a warm place until doubled in size – about 1 hour.

On a lightly-floured surface, knead the dough quickly, then place in an oiled 2 lb (900 g) loaf tin. Cover with oiled polythene and leave in a warm place until doubled in size – about 1 hour.

Bake at 425°F/220°C/gas mark 7 for 35–40 minutes. Cool on a wire tray.

Makes 1 loaf

SPIRAL ONION BREAD

Delicious served with soup.

Fresh yeast ½ oz (15 g)
Unrefined brown sugar 1 tsp (5 ml)
Water, tepid ½ pt (300 ml)
Wholemeal flour 1 lb (450 g)
Celery seeds 1 tbsp (15 ml)
Poppy seeds 1 tbsp (15 ml)
Salt 1½ tsp (7.5 ml)
Ground pepper ½ tsp (2.5 ml)
Egg glaze (see p. 92)

FILLING
Onion, finely chopped 1
Butter 1 oz (25 g)
Parmesan cheese, grated 2 oz (50 g)

Mix the yeast with the sugar and water. Leave in a warm place for about 10 minutes until frothy.

Place the remaining ingredients in a large bowl and add the yeast liquid. Mix to a soft dough, then knead for 8–10 minutes. Cover and leave on one side.

For the filling, sauté the onion in the butter until transparent. Leave to cool, then stir in the cheese.

On a lightly-floured surface, roll out the dough to an oblong about 15×12 in (38×30 cm) and spread the filling over the dough. Fold the long ends in by 1 in (2.5 cm) then roll up from a short edge and place on a baking tray.

Cover with oiled polythene and leave in a warm place for 30–45 minutes, until doubled in size.

Brush with egg glaze and bake at 425°F/220°C/gas mark 7 for 35–40 minutes. Cool on a wire tray.

Makes 1 loaf

ENGLISH MUFFINS

Sometimes known as oven-bottom cakes because that was the position in which they were baked. Muffins may also be cooked on a griddle.

Wholemeal flour 1¼ lb (550 g)
Salt 1 tsp (5 ml)
Unrefined brown sugar 1 oz (25 g)
Milk ½ pt (300 ml)
Butter 2 oz (50 g)
Fresh yeast ½ oz (15 g)
Free-range egg, beaten 1
Corn meal (maize flour) to sprinkle

Mix the flour, salt and sugar in a bowl. Warm the milk and butter until tepid, then stir in the yeast. Add the yeast mixture and beaten egg to the dry ingredients and mix well to make a soft dough.

Knead for about 5 minutes until smooth and elastic and no longer sticky. Cover the dough and leave in a warm place until doubled in size – about 1½ hours.

Knead the dough on a lightly-floured surface once more, then roll out about ½ in (1 cm) thick and stamp out 3 in (7.5 cm) rounds with a floured cutter. Sprinkle both sides of each muffin with the cornmeal, then place on buttered baking trays. Reroll the trimmings to shape more muffins.

Cover the muffins with oiled polythene and leave in a warm place until doubled in size – about 30 minutes.

Bake at 425°F/220°C/gas mark 7 for about 10 minutes, or cook on a lightly-oiled griddle for about 15 minutes, turning once. Cool on a wire tray.

Makes about 15

FOUR GRAIN HOAGIES

Rye flour 4 oz (100 g)
Barley flour 4 oz (100 g)
Wholemeal flour 4 oz (100 g)
Medium oatmeal 4 oz (100 g)
Salt 1 tsp (5 ml)
Fresh yeast 1 oz (25 g)
Unrefined brown sugar 1 tsp (5 ml)
Water, tepid 8 fl oz (250 ml)
Egg glaze (see p. 92)
Rye flakes to sprinkle

Place the flours, oatmeal and salt in a bowl. Mix the yeast, sugar and water with 2 tbsp (30 ml) of the flour and oatmeal mixture. Leave in a warm place until frothy – about 10 minutes.

Mix all the ingredients together and knead for 8–10 minutes.

Place the dough on a lightly-floured surface and divide into six equal portions. Shape each portion into a 6 in (15 cm) baton and place on a lightly-oiled baking tray. Cover with oiled polythene and leave in a warm place until doubled in size – about 1 hour.

Brush with egg glaze and sprinkle with rye flakes. Bake at 425°F/220°C/gas mark 7 for 15–20 minutes. Cool on a wire tray.

Makes 6

BAGELS

Wholemeal Bagels are a first for Cranks! Serve split and filled with cream cheese and walnuts.

Fresh yeast 1 oz (25 g)
Unrefined brown sugar 2 tsp (10 ml)
Water, tepid ¼ pt (150 ml)
Wholemeal flour 12 oz (350 g)
Salt ½ tsp (2.5 ml)
Free-range egg, beaten 1
Butter, melted 3 tbsp (45 ml)
Egg glaze (see p. 92)
Coarse salt or seeds such as poppy, cumin or aniseed to sprinkle

Mix the yeast, sugar and water together and leave in a warm place until frothy – about 10 minutes. Combine the flour and salt and add the yeast liquid, egg and melted butter. Knead for 8–10 minutes.

Place the dough on a lightly-floured surface and divide into 12 equal portions.

Shape each portion into an 8 in (20 cm) baton and form into a ring, sealing the ends together well with water. Place on a lightly-oiled baking tray and cover with oiled polythene. Leave in a warm place until doubled in size – 10–15 minutes.

Bring a large saucepan of water to the boil and carefully drop the bagels one at a time into the boiling water. Leave for 30 seconds until puffed up.

Remove from the pan, drain well and place on lightly-oiled baking trays. Brush with egg glaze and sprinkle with salt or seeds as desired.

Bake at 400°F/200°C/gas mark 6 for 20 minutes. Cool on a wire tray.

Makes 12

GREEN OLIVE GRISSINI

Crisp little bread sticks, speckled with green herbs and olives.

Fresh yeast ½ oz (15 g)
Unrefined brown sugar 1 tsp (5 ml)
Water, tepid ⅓ pt (200 ml)
Wholemeal flour 1 lb (450 g)
Salt 1 tsp (5 ml)
Ground pepper ½ tsp (2.5 ml)
Green olives, pitted 3 oz (75 g)
Onion 3 oz (75 g)
Fresh basil ½ oz (15 g)
Olive oil 1 tbsp (15 ml)

Mix the yeast, sugar and water and leave in a warm place until frothy – about 10 minutes.

Combine the flour, salt and pepper in a large bowl.

Very finely chop the olives, onion and basil together – or blend to a coarse purée in a food processor.

Add the yeast liquid, olive mixture and oil to the flour. Mix to a soft dough, then knead for 8–10 minutes. Divide the dough into 32 portions.

On a lightly-floured board, knead each portion quickly, then roll into a thin stick about 12 in (30 cm) long. Place the sticks on several oiled baking trays, cover with oiled polythene and leave for 30 minutes in a warm place.

Bake at 350°F/180°C/gas mark 4 for 30 minutes.

Makes 32

HERB & SESAME PITTA BREAD

Try pitta bread this way – it's fantastic!

Fresh yeast ½ oz (15 g)
Unrefined brown sugar 1 tsp (5 ml)
Water, tepid ½ pt (300 ml)
Wholemeal flour 1 lb (450 g)
Salt 1 tsp (5 ml)

TOPPING
Olive oil 6 tbsp (90 ml)
Fresh thyme, chopped 4 tbsp (60 ml)
Fresh marjoram, chopped 2 tbsp (30 ml)
Sesame seeds 2 tbsp (30 ml)

Mix the yeast, sugar and water and leave in a warm place until frothy – about 10 minutes.

Combine the flour and salt, add the yeast liquid and mix to a soft dough. Knead for 8–10 minutes.

Place the dough in an oiled bowl, cover with oiled polythene and leave in a warm place until doubled in size – about 1 hour.

On a lightly-floured surface, knead the dough quickly, then divide into eight portions. Knead each portion into a small ball, then roll out to about ⅛–¼ in (3–6 mm). Cover each piece with oiled polythene and leave to rest for 30 minutes.

Combine the ingredients for the topping. Heat the oven to 450°F/230°C/gas mark 8 and warm several baking trays.

One at a time, brush the baking trays with oil, position the pieces of dough and spread liberally with the herb topping. Bake for about 8 minutes until risen and puffed.

Makes 8

STEAMED RYE BREAD WITH ALMONDS

Delicious sliced and spread with cream cheese or butter.

Wholemeal flour 4 oz (100 g)
Rye flour 4 oz (100 g)
Semolina 4 oz (100 g)
Baking powder 1½ tsp (7.5 ml)
Salt 1 tsp (5 ml)
Ground nutmeg ½ tsp (2.5 ml)
Ground cinnamon ½ tsp (2.5 ml)
Unrefined brown sugar 1 oz (25 g)
Almonds, chopped or flaked 2 oz (50 g)
Black treacle 8 tbsp (120 ml)
Milk ⅔ pt (400 ml)
Lemon juice 4 tsp (20 ml)

Mix together the flours, semolina, baking powder, salt, spices and sugar. Add the almonds, black treacle, milk and lemon juice and beat well until evenly mixed.

Generously butter a 2¼ pt (1.3 l) decorative tin and pour in the mixture. Cover with foil, sealing the edges tightly.

Steam the bread for 2 hours until firm and risen. Cool on a wire tray.

Makes 1 loaf

CORIANDER & CARAWAY FLATS

Cut these spicy flats into wedges and use as a base for open sandwiches.

Fresh yeast 1 oz (25 g)
Unrefined brown sugar 1 tsp (5 ml)
Water, tepid ¾ pt (450 ml)
Rye flour 13 oz (375 g)
Wholemeal flour 13 oz (375 g)
Salt 1 tsp (5 ml)
Caraway seeds 2 tsp (10 ml)
Coriander seeds, crushed 2 tsp (10 ml)

Mix the yeast, sugar and water and leave in a warm place until frothy – about 10 minutes.

Combine the flours, salt and seeds. Add the yeast liquid and mix to a soft dough. Knead for 8–10 minutes.

Transfer to a lightly-floured surface and divide into four portions. Lightly knead each portion and roll out to an 8 in (20 cm) round. Place on oiled baking trays, cover with oiled polythene and leave in a warm place for 30–45 minutes until doubled in size.

Bake at 425°F/220°C/gas mark 7 for 15–20 minutes. Cool on a wire tray.

Makes 4

Sunflower & Honey Bread, page 26
Spoon Bread, page 33
Kibbled Wheat Cobs, page 29
Green Olive Grissini, page 45
Oatmeal & Treacle Bread, page 28

Apple & Sunflower Scones, page 64
Coriander & Caraway Flats, page 48
French Walnut Bread, page 31
Steamed Rye Bread with Almonds, page 47
Pecan Waffles, page 60

Nutter Spiral Cake, page 77
Syrup Doughnuts, page 68
Pear, Ginger & Sultana Braid, page 85
Lemon & Plum Doughnuts, page 67
Plum Pizza Streusel, page 86

Brewery Bread, page 22
Garlic & Herb Sticks, page 37
Wholemeal Crumpets, page 53
Pumpkin Bread, page 35
Italian Style Tomato Bread, page 73

Multi-Seed Bread, page 32
Cheese Scones, page 52
English Muffins, page 42
Brioche Loaf, page 75
Potato Soda Bread, page 34
Herb & Sesame Pitta Bread, page 46

Herbed Potato Baps, page 50
Bagels, page 44
Four-Grain Hoagies, page 43
Selection of Wholemeal Rolls, page 13, 17

MILLET, CARROT & RAISIN LOAF

Grind your own millet seeds in a coffee grinder for this tasty gluten-free bread. It is well worth the effort!

Millet seeds 6 oz (175 g)
Carrot, finely grated 6 oz (175 g)
Raisins 3 oz (75 g)
Salt 1 tsp (5 ml)
Honey 1 tbsp (15 ml)
Oil 2 tbsp (30 ml)
Water, boiling 6 fl oz (175 ml)
Free-range eggs, separated 2

Grind the millet seeds to a fine flour and combine with the grated carrot, raisins, salt and honey. Add the oil and boiling water and mix well.

Beat in the egg yolks. Stiffly whisk the egg whites and fold into the mixture. Transfer to an oiled and base-lined 1 lb (450 g) loaf tin and bake at 350°F/180°C/gas mark 4 for 45 minutes until risen and firm to the touch.

Cool on a wire tray.

Makes 1 loaf

HERBED POTATO BAPS

Perfect for picnics!

Fresh yeast 1 oz (25 g)
Unrefined brown sugar 1 tsp (5 ml)
Milk, tepid ⅓ pt (200 ml)
Wholemeal flour 12 oz (350 g)
Salt 1 tsp (5 ml)
Dried mixed herbs 1 tsp (5 ml)
Spring onions, trimmed and chopped 4
Cheddar cheese, grated 2 oz (50 g)
Potato, cooked and mashed 8 oz (225 g)
Egg glaze (see p. 92)

Combine the yeast, sugar and milk and leave in a warm place until frothy – about 10 minutes.

Place the flour, salt, herbs, spring onions, cheese and mashed potato in a bowl. Add the yeast liquid and knead for 5 minutes. Place the dough on a lightly-floured surface and divide into six portions. Shape each portion into a round, place on a lightly-oiled baking tray, cover with oiled polythene and leave in a warm place until doubled in size – about 20 minutes. Brush with egg glaze.

Bake at 425°F/220°C/gas mark 7 for 20–25 minutes. Cool on a wire tray.

Makes 6

CRANKS CHEESE BAPS

A 25-year favourite which won the *Evening Standard* award for the best sandwich in London.

Serve split and buttered with mustard and cress or alfalfa sprouts.

Fresh yeast ½ oz (15 g)
Unrefined brown sugar 1 tsp (5 ml)
Water, tepid ½ pt (300 ml)
Wholemeal flour 1 lb (450 g)
Salt 1 tsp (5 ml)
Cheddar cheese, grated 9 oz (275 g)
Milk to glaze

Mix the yeast, sugar and water and leave in a warm place until frothy – about 10 minutes.

Combine the flour and salt in a large bowl, add the yeast liquid and mix to a soft dough. Knead for 8–10 minutes. On a lightly-floured surface, roll the dough to a 15×10 in (38×25 cm) oblong. Divide the grated cheese into three portions. Mark the dough into three sections as below and sprinkle one third of the cheese over the centre section (2). Fold (1) over (2) and seal the edges by pressing firmly with a rolling pin. Sprinkle a portion of the cheese over the double thickness of dough (1 & 2) and fold over section (3). Seal the edges with a rolling pin.

15 in (38 cm)

1	2	3

10 in (25 cm)

Roll out the dough to about ¾ in (2 cm) thick and stamp out 4 in (10 cm) rounds. Reroll as required. Place on a lightly-oiled baking tray and brush with milk. Sprinkle with the remaining cheese.

Cover with oiled polythene and leave in a warm place for 30 minutes. Bake at 400°F/200°C/gas mark 6 for about 25 minutes. Cool on a wire tray.

Makes 6–8

CHEESE SCONES

Wholemeal flour 1 lb (450 g)
Baking powder 2 tbsp (30 ml)
Salt ½ tsp (2.5 ml)
Cayenne ½ tsp (2.5 ml)
Butter 2 oz (50 g)
Cheddar cheese, grated 8–10 oz (225–300 g)
Milk ½ pt (300 ml)
Egg glaze, optional (see p. 92)

Mix the flour, baking powder, salt and cayenne in a bowl. Rub in the butter until the mixture resembles fine crumbs, stir in the cheese and mix to a soft dough with the milk.

Knead on a lightly-floured surface and roll out 1 in (2.5 cm) thick. Stamp out 3 in (7.5 cm) rounds with a fluted cutter and place close together on a buttered baking tray.

Brush with egg glaze and bake at 425°F/220°C/gas mark 7 for about 20 minutes until risen and golden.

Cool on a wire tray.

Makes 14

WHOLEMEAL CRUMPETS

Good crumpets are difficult to make, but this recipe proves it can be done!

85% wholemeal flour 1 lb (450 g)
Salt 2 tsp (10 ml)
Water ¾pt (450 ml)
Milk ½ pt (300 ml)
Oil 2 tbsp (30 ml)
Fresh yeast ½ oz (15 g)
Unrefined brown sugar 1 tsp (5 ml)
Bicarbonate of soda ½ tsp (2.5 ml)

Combine the flour and salt in a bowl. Warm ½ pt (300 ml) of the water, the milk and the oil in a saucepan until tepid. Stir in the yeast and sugar; add to the flour. Beat well.

Cover with cling film and leave in a warm place for 2 hours.

Heat the remaining water in a saucepan until tepid. Stir in the bicarbonate of soda and beat into the flour mixture to make a smooth batter. Cover and leave in a warm place for 30 minutes.

Place a buttered griddle or large frying pan over a medium heat and put five buttered crumpet rings on it. Pour 4 tbsp (60 ml) of the batter into each crumpet ring and cook for 10 minutes until completely set.

Carefully remove the crumpet rings and turn the crumpets over. Cook for a further 2 minutes. Repeat until all the batter is used up.

Cool on a wire tray.

Best eaten toasted and buttered.

Makes about 20

WHOLEMEAL CRESCENTS

Wholemeal flour 1 lb (450 g)
Salt 1 tsp (5 ml)
Nutter 2 oz (50 g)
Fresh yeast 1 oz (25 g)
Water, tepid 8 fl oz (250 ml)
Free-range egg, beaten 1
Butter, softened 6 oz (175 g)
Unrefined brown sugar ½ tsp (2.5 ml)

GLAZE
Free-range egg, beaten 1
Unrefined brown sugar ½ tsp (2.5 ml)
Water 2 tsp (10 ml)

Mix the flour and salt together and rub in the nutter. Mix the yeast with the water and add with the beaten egg to the dry ingredients and work to a smooth soft dough. Knead on a lightly-floured surface for about 10 minutes.

Roll out to a rectangle 20×8 in (50×20 cm), divide the butter into three portions. Dot one portion of butter over two thirds of the dough, leaving a 1 in (2.5 cm) border around the edges.

Fold the dough in three by folding the unbuttered portion over half the buttered portion, then fold the opposite buttered side on top. Seal the edges firmly with a rolling pin; then repeat the rolling out twice more adding one portion of butter each time.

Wrap the dough in cling film or oiled polythene and leave for at least 30 minutes. Roll out and fold three more times but without adding any butter.

Cover and chill for at least 1 hour. On a lightly-floured surface, roll out the dough to a rectangle 24×14 in (60×35 cm). Trim the edges and cut in half lengthways. Cut each strip into triangles (as shown).

Join the end pieces to make two more triangles. Beat the glaze ingredients together and brush over each triangle, then roll up loosely from the long edge. Place on a baking sheet and curve into crescent shapes.

Cover with oiled polythene and leave in a warm place for 30 minutes or until springy to the touch. Brush with the egg glaze and bake at 425°F/220°C/gas mark 7 for 15–20 minutes. Cool on a wire tray.

Makes 12

Variation
Carob
Prepare the dough exactly as above and cut into triangles. Place two squares of carob bar on the long edge of each triangle before shaping. Bake as above.

Cheese
Prepare the dough exactly as above and cut into triangles. Omit the sugar from the glaze and add a pinch of salt. Place a 1 oz (25 g) baton of mature Cheddar cheese on the long edge of each triangle before shaping. Bake as above.

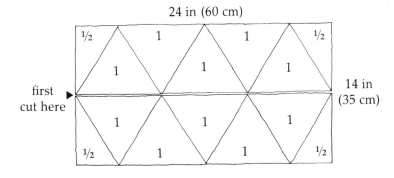

DANISH PASTRIES

Wholemeal flour 1 lb (450 g)
Salt 1 tsp (5 ml)
Nutter 2 oz (50 g)
Fresh yeast 1 oz (25 g)
Milk, tepid 8 fl oz (250 ml)
Free-range egg, beaten 1
Butter, softened 6 oz (175 g)

GLAZE
Free-range egg, beaten 1
Water 2 tsp (10 ml)
Unrefined brown sugar ½ tsp (2.5 ml)
Fillings (see p. 59)
Apricot jam, warmed and sieved to glaze

Mix the flour and salt together and rub in the nutter. Mix the yeast with the milk and add with the beaten egg to the dry ingredients and work to a smooth dough. Knead on a lightly-floured surface for about 10 minutes.

Roll out to a rectangle 20×8 in (50×20 cm), divide the butter into three portions. Dot one portion of butter over two-thirds of the dough, leaving a 1 in (2.5 cm) border around the edges.

Fold the dough in three by folding the unbuttered portion over half the buttered portion, then fold the opposite buttered side on top. Seal the edges firmly with a rolling pin, then repeat the rolling out twice more, adding a portion of butter each time.

Wrap the dough in cling film or oiled polythene and chill for at least 30 minutes. Roll out and fold three more times but without adding any butter.

Cover and chill for at least 1 hour. On a lightly floured surface roll out the dough to a rectangle

24×16 in (60×40 cm) and cut into twenty-four 4 in (10 cm) squares.

To shape combs
Place 1 oz (25 g) almond filling on one side of each square. Brush the edges with glaze, fold over and seal well. Cut through the dough several times to shape the comb.

Place on a buttered baking tray and curve each comb to fan out slightly. Cover with oiled polythene and leave in a warm place for 30 minutes. Brush with glaze and sprinkle with flaked almonds, if wished.

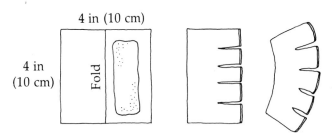

To shape windmills
Place 1 oz (25 g) almond filling in the centre of each square. Make a cut from the filling to each corner. Brush the dough with glaze and draw up the dough at each corner (as marked below) to form a windmill.

Place on a buttered baking tray. Cover with oiled polythene and leave in a warm place for 30 minutes. Brush with glaze.

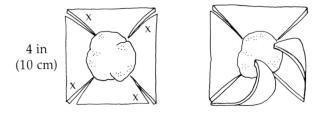

To shape envelopes
Place 1 oz (25 g) cinnamon filling or carob bar in the centre of each square. Brush the edges of the dough with glaze and draw in the corners and fold, sealing the edges thoroughly.

4 in (10 cm)

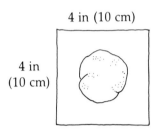

4 in
(10 cm)

Place on a buttered baking tray. Cover with oiled polythene and leave in a warm place for 30 minutes. Brush with glaze.

To shape boats
Place 1 oz (25 g) almond filling in the centre of each square. Brush edges with glaze. Fold over opposite corners.

4 in (10 cm)

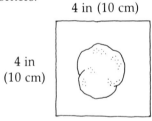

4 in
(10 cm)

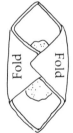

Place on buttered baking tray. Cover with oiled polythene and leave in a warm place for 30 minutes. Brush with glaze.

Bake all pastries at 425°F/220°C/gas mark 7 for 15–20 minutes until golden. Brush with sieved and warmed apricot jam; leave to cool on a wire tray.

Makes 24

FILLING FOR DANISH PASTRIES

ALMOND
Ground almonds 4 oz (100 g)
Unrefined brown sugar 2 tbsp (30 ml)
Egg white 1
Natural almond essence, a few drops

Mix all the ingredients together until evenly combined.

Makes 6 oz (175 g)

CINNAMON BUTTER
Butter, softened 3 oz (75 g)
Unrefined brown sugar 3 oz (75 g)
Ground cinnamon 1 tbsp (15 ml)

Beat the butter, sugar and cinnamon together until evenly combined. Place on a piece of greaseproof paper or foil and roll into a neat shape.

Chill until firm.

Makes 6 oz (175 g)

PECAN WAFFLES

Serve fresh or toasted with maple syrup, ice cream
and strawberries.

Fresh yeast ½ oz (15 g)
Unrefined brown sugar 1 oz (25 g)
Milk, tepid 6 fl oz (175 ml)
85% wholemeal flour 6 oz (175 g)
Salt ¼ tsp (1.25 ml)
Lemon, finely grated rind of ½
Butter, melted 2 oz (50 g)
Free-range eggs, beaten 2
Pecans, finely chopped 2 oz (50 g)

Mix the yeast, sugar and milk and leave in a warm
place for about 10 minutes until frothy.

Place the remaining ingredients in a large bowl.
Add the yeast liquid and beat to a thick batter.

Cover and leave in a warm place for 30 minutes.

Thoroughly oil a 7 in (18 cm) waffle iron and place
over a medium heat until warmed. Spoon about one
fifth of the batter into the waffle iron and close the lid.
Cook for about 2 minutes each side, until golden
brown.

Repeat with the remaining mixture.

Makes 5

FRUIT SCONES

Wholemeal flour 1 lb (450 g)
Baking powder 2 tbsp (30 ml)
Unrefined brown sugar 3 oz (75 g)
Butter 4 oz (100 g)
Currants or sultanas 3 oz (75 g)
Milk ⅓ pt (200 ml)
Egg glaze, optional (see p. 92)

Mix the flour, baking powder and sugar together in a bowl. Rub in the butter until the mixture resembles fine crumbs. Stir in the currants and mix to a soft dough with the milk.

Knead gently on a lightly-floured surface and roll out 1 in (2.5 cm) thick. Stamp out 2½ in (6.5 cm) rounds with a fluted cutter and place close together on a buttered baking tray.

Brush with egg glaze and bake at 425°F/220°C/gas mark 7 for 15–20 minutes until risen and golden.

Cool on a wire tray.

Variation
Replace the currants or sultanas with an equal quantity of chopped dried dates.

Makes about 15

TREACLE SCONES

Wholemeal self-raising flour 1 lb (450 g)
Salt, a pinch
Bicarbonate of soda 1 tsp (5 ml)
Ground mixed spice 1 tbsp (15 ml)
Unrefined brown sugar 2 oz (50 g)
Butter 4 oz (100 g)
Black treacle 4 tbsp (60 ml)
Milk ⅓ pt (200 ml)
Egg glaze (see p. 92)

Mix together the flour, salt, bicarbonate of soda, spice and sugar. Rub in the butter until the mixture resembles fine crumbs.

Stir together the black treacle and milk and add to the dry ingredients. Mix to a soft dough.

Roll out on a lightly-floured surface to about 1 in (2.5 cm) thickness. Stamp out 3 in (7.5 cm) rounds and place close together on a buttered baking tray. Brush with egg glaze and bake at 425°F/220°C/gas mark 7 for 15–20 minutes until risen and firm to the touch.

Cool on a wire tray.

Variation
Add 3 oz (75 g) chopped dried fruit before adding the liquid.

Makes 12–14

CAROB CHIP & GINGER SCONES

Wholemeal flour 1 lb (450 g)
Baking powder 2 tbsp (30 ml)
Butter 4 oz (100 g)
Unrefined brown sugar 3 oz (75 g)
Carob chips 2 oz (50 g)
Crystallized ginger, finely chopped 1 oz (25 g)
Milk ⅓ pt (200 ml)
Egg glaze (see p. 92)

Combine the flour and baking powder in a bowl and rub in the butter. Stir in the sugar, carob chips and chopped ginger and add the milk to form a soft dough. Transfer to a lightly floured surface and knead quickly. Roll out the dough 1 in (2.5 cm) thick, and with a 2½ in (6.5 cm) plain pastry cutter, stamp out scones and place on a buttered baking tray.

Alternatively, arrange the scones, overlapping in a circle.

Brush with egg glaze and bake at 425°F/220°C/gas mark 7 for 15–20 minutes until risen and golden.

Cool on a wire tray.

Makes about 14

APPLE & SUNFLOWER SCONES

Wholemeal flour 1 lb (450 g)
Baking powder 2 tbsp (30 ml)
Butter 4 oz (100 g)
Unrefined brown sugar 3 oz (75 g)
Sunflower seeds 1 oz (25 g)
Medium dessert apple, cored and finely chopped 1
Milk ⅓ pt (200 ml)
Egg glaze (see p. 92)

Combine the flour and baking powder in a bowl and rub in the butter. Stir in the sugar, sunflower seeds and apple and add the milk to form a soft dough.

Transfer to a lightly-floured surface and knead quickly.

Roll out the dough 1 in (2.5 cm) thick and, using a 2½ in (6.5 cm) plain cutter, stamp out rounds. Place close together on a buttered baking tray.

Brush with egg glaze and bake at 425°F/220°C/gas mark 7 for 15–20 minutes until risen and golden.

Cool on a wire tray.

Makes about 14

DROP SCONES

Wholemeal flour 8 oz (225 g)
Salt ½ tsp (2.5 ml)
Unrefined brown sugar 2 oz (50 g)
Cream of tartar 1 tsp (5 ml)
Bicarbonate of soda ½ tsp (2.5 ml)
Lemon, finely grated rind of 1
Free-range egg, beaten 1
Milk ½ pt (300 ml)

Mix the flour, salt, sugar, cream of tartar and bicarbonate of soda in a bowl. Make a hole in the centre and beat in the lemon rind, egg and milk to give a smooth thick batter.

Butter a griddle or large frying pan and place over a medium heat. When hot, drop tablespoons (15 ml) of mixture evenly spaced onto the griddle. Cook for about 5 minutes, turning once until golden brown and risen.

Serve warm with butter.

Makes about 27

SULTANA MUFFINS

Muffins are best served fresh from the oven.

Butter 2 oz (50 g)
Wholemeal self-raising flour 6 oz (175 g)
Ground cinnamon 1 tsp (5 ml)
Unrefined brown sugar 1 oz (25 g)
Sultanas 3 oz (75 g)
Free-range egg, beaten 1
Milk 4 fl oz (100 ml)

Rub the butter into the flour. Stir in the cinnamon, sugar and sultanas. Mix the beaten egg and milk and stir quickly into the dry ingredients. Divide the mixture between eight buttered muffin tins and bake at 375°F/190°C/gas mark 5 for 20 minutes until risen and firm to the touch. Cool on a wire tray.

Variation
Blueberry
Substitute 3 oz (75 g) blueberries for the sultanas.

Carob
Substitute 3 oz (75 g) carob chips for the sultanas.

Makes 8

GRIDDLE CAKES

Best served fresh from the griddle!

Fresh yeast ½ oz (15 g)
Milk, tepid 6 fl oz (175 ml)
Wholemeal flour 8 oz (225 g)
Unrefined brown sugar 2 oz (50 g)
Currants 2 oz (50 g)
Sultanas 2 oz (50 g)
Salt, a pinch
Ground pepper, a pinch
Ground nutmeg, a pinch
Ground cinnamon, a pinch
Free-range egg, beaten 1

Mix the yeast and milk together and leave in a warm place for about 10 minutes until frothy.

Combine the flour, sugar, fruit, salt and spices. Add the yeast liquid and egg and mix to a thick batter.

Cover and leave in a warm place for 1 hour. Beat well and add a little extra warm milk if necessary.

Drop spoonfuls of the batter on to a buttered griddle or large frying pan and cook for 8–10 minutes, turning once. Repeat until all the mixture is used up.

Serve warm.

Makes about 18

LEMON & PLUM DOUGHNUTS

Irresistible!

Fresh yeast ½ oz (15 g)
Milk, tepid 4 fl oz (100 ml)
Unrefined brown sugar 1 oz (25 g)
Wholemeal flour 8 oz (225 g)
Salt ¼ tsp (1.25 ml)
Free-range egg, beaten 1
Butter, melted 2 oz (50 g)
Lemon, finely grated rind of ½
Plum jam 8 tsp (40 ml)
Oil for deep frying
Unrefined caster sugar to sprinkle

Mix the yeast, milk and sugar together and leave in a warm place until frothy – about 10 minutes.

Mix the flour and salt together. Add the yeast liquid, egg, butter and lemon rind and beat to a soft dough. Cover and leave in a warm place for 30 minutes.

Transfer to a lightly-floured surface and knead quickly. Divide the dough into eight portions and flatten each one to a round. Place a teaspoon of jam in the centre of each, then draw up the edges of the dough to encase the jam completely, sealing it well.

Place the shaped doughnuts on a baking tray and leave to rise for 15 minutes, or until doubled in size.

Heat the oil to 350–360°F/175–180°C on a sugar thermometer and fry the doughnuts in two batches, for about 6 minutes, turning once, until golden brown.

Drain on absorbent paper and toss in caster sugar while still warm.

Makes 8

SYRUP DOUGHNUTS

Sticky and wicked!

Fresh yeast ½ oz (15 g)
Unrefined brown sugar 1 oz (25 g)
Milk, tepid 4 fl oz (100 ml)
Wholemeal flour 8 oz (225 g)
Salt ¼ tsp (1.25 ml)
Ground almonds 2 oz (50 g)
Lemon, finely grated rind of ½
Free-range egg, beaten 1
Butter, melted 2 oz (50 g)
Oil for deep frying
Pistachio nuts, chopped ½ oz (15 g)

SYRUP
Unrefined light brown sugar 4 oz (100 g)
Honey 2 oz (50 g)
Water 4 tbsp (60 ml)
Lemon juice 1 tbsp (15 ml)

Mix the yeast, sugar and milk and leave in a warm place until frothy – about 10 minutes.

Combine the flour, salt and ground almonds. Add the yeast liquid, lemon rind, egg and butter and mix to a soft dough.

Cover and leave in a warm place for 30 minutes.

Transfer the dough to a lightly-floured surface and divide into 16 portions. Roll each one into a baton about 8 in (20 cm) long and tie each baton in a knot. Cover and leave in a warm place for 15 minutes, or until doubled in size.

Heat the oil to 350–360°F/175–180°C on a sugar thermometer and cook the doughnuts in two batches for 3–4 minutes, turning as necessary.

Drain on absorbent paper.

For the syrup, place all the ingredients in a saucepan and boil for 5 minutes. Pour over the doughnuts and leave to soak. Sprinkle with chopped pistachio nuts.

Makes 16

ONION·PIZZA

A cross between a pizza and a quiche.

DOUGH
Fresh yeast ½ oz (15 g)
Unrefined brown sugar ½ tsp (2.5 ml)
Water, tepid ¼ pt (150 ml)
Wholemeal flour 8 oz (225 g)
Salt ½ tsp (2.5 ml)
Oil 1 tsp (5 ml)

TOPPING
Butter 1 oz (25 g)
Onions, thinly sliced 2 lb (900 g)
Soured cream ¼ pt (150 ml)
Free-range egg, beaten 1
Caraway seeds 1 tbsp (15 ml)
Salt and pepper to taste

Mix the yeast, sugar and water together and leave in a warm place until frothy – about 10 minutes.

Combine the flour and salt, add the yeast liquid and mix to a soft dough. Knead for 8–10 minutes, then transfer to a lightly floured surface. Roll out and use to line an 11 in (28 cm) pizza tray. Brush with oil and leave to prove for 30 minutes.

For the topping, melt the butter and sweat the onions for 25–30 minutes until very soft. Add the remaining ingredients and season generously.

Spread the onion mixture over the dough and bake at 400°F/200°C/gas mark 6 for 25–30 minutes.

Serves 4–6

SICILIAN TOMATO PIZZAS

TOPPING
Tomatoes, finely chopped 1 lb (450 g)
Garlic clove, finely chopped 1
Small onion, finely chopped 1
Salt ½ tsp (2.5 ml)
Olive oil 2 tbsp (30 ml)
Black olives, pitted and chopped 12
Dried oregano 1 tsp (5 ml)
Parmesan cheese, grated 2 oz (50 g)
Freshly ground black pepper to sprinkle

DOUGH
Fresh yeast ½ oz (15 g)
Unrefined brown sugar 1 tbsp (15 ml)
Water, tepid ¼ pt (150 ml)
Wholemeal flour 6 oz (175 g)
Soya flour 2 oz (50 g)
Salt ½ tsp (2.5 ml)
Oil 2 tbsp (30 ml)

For the topping, combine the tomatoes, garlic, onion, salt, oil, olives and oregano. Cover and leave to marinate.

For the dough, mix the yeast, sugar and water; leave in a warm place for about 10 minutes until frothy. Combine the flours and salt, add the yeast liquid and oil; knead for 8–10 minutes. Transfer to a lightly-floured surface and cut into four portions. Knead each one to a round, then roll out to about 5 in (12.5 cm) diameter.

Place on a lightly-oiled baking tray. Leave to rest for 30 minutes. Divide the tomato mixture between the rounds of dough, level the surface and sprinkle with the Parmesan cheese. Bake at 425°F/220°C/gas mark 7 for about 20 minutes until bubbling and golden. Serve warm, sprinkled with black pepper.

Makes 4

SPINACH CALZONE

A giant folded pizza! Serve it warm.

Filling: *Butter 1 oz (25 g)*
Onion, chopped 1
Spinach, shredded 1 lb (450 g)
Mushrooms, chopped 4 oz (100 g)
Dried thyme ½ tsp (2.5 ml)
Ground nutmeg, a generous pinch
Cottage cheese 4 oz (100 g)
Pine kernels 1 oz (25 g)
Salt and pepper to taste

Dough: *Fresh yeast ½ oz (15 g)*
Unrefined brown sugar ½ tsp (2.5 ml)
Water, tepid ¼ pt (150 ml)
Wholemeal flour 8 oz (225 g)
Salt and oil ½ tsp (2.5 ml) of each
Parmesan cheese, grated 2 tbsp (30 ml)

For the filling, melt the butter in a large saucepan and sauté the onion until transparent. Add the spinach, stir until wilted, add the mushrooms, thyme and nutmeg and cook until there is no free liquid. Cool slightly. Mix in the remaining ingredients.

For the dough, mix the yeast, sugar and water together and leave in a warm place until frothy – about 10 minutes. Combine the flour and salt; add the yeast liquid and mix to a soft dough. Knead for 8–10 minutes. Roll out the dough on a lightly floured surface to a 12 in (30 cm) round. Spread the spinach filling over one half of the dough. Brush the edges with water, fold the dough over the filling and seal well. Brush with the oil and sprinkle with the Parmesan cheese. Prick the top of the dough and transfer to a lightly-oiled baking tray, cover with oiled polythene; leave in a warm place for 30 minutes. Bake at 400°F/200°C/gas mark 6 for 30 minutes.
Serves 4

CRANKS TRADITIONAL PIZZA

SAUCE
Oil 1 tbsp (15 ml)
Onions, chopped 8 oz (225 g)
Garlic clove, crushed 1
Tomato purée 1 tbsp (15 ml)
Dried basil ¼ tsp (1.25 ml)
Dried oregano ¼ tsp (1.25 ml)
Dried mixed herbs ¼ tsp (1.25 ml)
Ground bayleaf ¼ tsp (1.25 ml)
Dried rosemary ¼ tsp (1.25 ml)
Tomatoes, chopped 1½ lb (675 g)
Salt and pepper to taste

DOUGH
Fresh yeast ½ oz (15 g)
Unrefined brown sugar ½ tsp (2.5 ml)
Water, tepid ¼ pt (150 ml)
Wholemeal flour 8 oz (225 g)
Salt ½ tsp (2.5 ml)
Oil 1 tsp (5 ml)

TOPPING
Tomatoes, sliced 2 oz (50 g)
Mushrooms, sliced 2 oz (50 g)
Green pepper, thinly sliced 2 oz (50 g)
Cheddar cheese, grated 6 oz (175 g)
Black olives 6
Dried oregano ½ tsp (2.5 ml)
Spring onions, chopped to garnish

For the sauce, heat the oil and sauté the onions and garlic. Add the tomato purée and herbs and cook slowly for 5 minutes. Add the tomatoes and season generously. Cook over medium heat, stirring occasionally, for about 30 minutes until thick. Leave to cool.

For the dough, mix the yeast, sugar and water and

leave in a warm place for about 10 minutes until frothy. Combine the flour and salt, then add the yeast liquid and mix to a soft dough. Knead for 8–10 minutes, then transfer to a lightly floured surface. Roll out and use to line an 11 in (28 cm) pizza tray. Brush with oil and leave to prove for 30 minutes. Spread the tomato sauce evenly over the dough and scatter the ingredients for the topping over the sauce.

Bake at 400°F/200°C/gas mark 6 for 25–30 minutes.

Serves 4–6

ITALIAN STYLE TOMATO BREAD

Tomato juice ½ pt (300 ml)
Fresh yeast ½ oz (15 g)
Unrefined brown sugar 1 tsp (5 ml)
Wholemeal flour 1 lb (450 g)
Salt 1 tsp (5 ml)
Ground pepper ½ tsp (2.5 ml)

Topping: *Olive oil 4 tbsp (60 ml)*
Tomato paste 4 tbsp (60 ml)
Fresh rosemary, chopped 2 tbsp (30 ml)

Warm the tomato juice until just tepid, then mix with the yeast and sugar. Leave in a warm place for about 10 minutes until frothy. Mix the flour, salt and pepper in a large bowl. Add the yeast liquid and mix to a soft dough. Knead for 8–10 minutes.

On a lightly-floured surface, roll out the dough and use to line a 13×9 in (33×23 cm) Swiss roll tin. Prick the surface with a fork. Combine the ingredients for the topping and spread over the dough. Cover with oiled polythene and leave in a warm place for 30 minutes.

Bake at 425°F/220°C/gas mark 7 for 15–20 minutes. Serve cut into squares.

Makes 15 squares

LEEKS & CHEESE
IN A BREAD CRUST

Fresh yeast ½ oz (15 g)
Unrefined brown sugar 1 tsp (5 ml)
Water, tepid ½ pt (300 ml)
Wholemeal flour 1 lb (450 g)
Salt 1 tsp (5 ml)

Filling: *Leeks, sliced 1½ lb (675 g)*
Butter 2 oz (50 g)
Cayenne, a generous pinch
Ground nutmeg, a generous pinch
Free-range eggs 6
Milk ½ pt (300 ml)
Soured cream ¼ pt (150 ml)
Salt, a generous pinch
Cheddar cheese, grated 12 oz (350 g)

Mix the yeast, sugar and water and leave in a warm place until frothy – about 10 minutes. Combine the flour and salt and add the yeast liquid. Mix to a soft dough, then knead for 8–10 minutes. Cover and leave to one side.

For the filling, thoroughly wash the leek slices and dry them on a kitchen cloth. Melt the butter and sauté the leeks, season generously with cayenne and nutmeg. Whisk the eggs, milk, soured cream and salt.

On a lightly-floured surface, roll the dough into a large rectangle and use to line a 12×9×2 in deep (30×23×5 cm) tin. Prick with a fork.

Sprinkle half the cheese on the base of the dough. Scatter the leek mixture on top, then pour in the egg custard. Scatter the remaining cheese on top and bake at 400°F/200°C/gas mark 6 for 1 hour until the filling is set and golden.

Serves 8–12

BRIOCHE LOAF

Fresh yeast ½ oz (15 g)
Milk, tepid 2 fl oz (50 ml)
Wholemeal flour 8 oz (225 g)
Unrefined brown sugar 1 oz (25 g)
Salt, a pinch
Free-range eggs, beaten 2
Butter, softened 4 oz (100 g)
Beaten egg to glaze

Mix the yeast and milk with a little of the flour to make a smooth paste. Leave in a warm place for about 10 minutes until frothy.

Add the remaining flour, sugar, salt and eggs and beat until smooth. Beat in the butter and continue working the dough until it starts to become elastic. Cover and leave in a warm place until doubled in size – about 1 hour.

Knead the dough on a lightly-floured surface, then divide into eight even-sized pieces. Shape each one into a ball.

Arrange the balls of dough in pairs along the length of a buttered 1 lb (450 g) loaf tin. Cover with oiled polythene and leave in a warm place until doubled in size – about 30–45 minutes.

Brush with beaten egg and bake at 425°F/220°C/ gas mark 7 for about 35 minutes until risen and firm to the touch. Cool on a wire tray.

Makes 1 loaf

Variations
Reserve one quarter of the dough. Shape the large portion of dough into a neat round and place in a buttered 8 in (20 cm) brioche mould. Make a large hole in the centre. Shape the small portion of dough

into a pear shape and place pointed side down on the hole. Cover and leave to rise. Glaze and bake as brioche loaf.

Makes 1 loaf

Alternatively, halve the dough and shape as above but use two 6 in (15 cm) brioche tins. Bake for 20–25 minutes.

Makes 2 loaves

Divide the dough into eight balls and place each ball of dough in individual buttered brioche moulds. Cover and leave in a warm place until doubled in size – about 30 minutes. Brush with beaten egg and bake at 425°F/220°C/gas mark 7 for 15–20 minutes. Cool on a wire tray.

Makes 8

Reserve one quarter of the dough. Shape this into eight small balls. Then shape the remaining dough into eight larger balls. Place a large ball of dough in individual buttered brioche moulds. Make a hole in the centre and place a small ball of dough on top. Cover and leave in a warm place until doubled in size – about 30 minutes. Brush with beaten egg and bake at 425°F/220°C/gas mark 7 for 15–20 minutes. Cool on a wire tray.

Makes 8

NUTTER SPIRAL CAKE

A spiral of sweetened bread stuffed with spice and raisins.

Fresh yeast 1½ oz (40 g)
Unrefined brown sugar 2 oz (50 g)
Milk, tepid 6 fl oz (175 ml)
Wholemeal flour 1 lb (450 g)
Salt 1 tsp (5 ml)
Free-range egg, beaten 1
Nutter, melted 2 oz (50 g)
Honey 4 tbsp (60 ml)

Filling: *Nutter, melted 4 oz (100 g)*
Unrefined brown sugar 4 oz (100 g)
Ground almonds 2 oz (50 g)
Ground cinnamon 1 tbsp (15 ml)
Raisins 6 oz (175 g)

Mix the yeast, 1 tsp (5 ml) of the sugar and the milk and leave in a warm place for about 10 minutes until frothy. Combine the flour, remaining sugar and salt in a bowl. Add the yeast liquid, egg and nutter and mix to a soft dough. Knead for 5 minutes, then transfer to a lightly-floured surface. Roll out to a rectangle 18×14 in (45×35 cm). Combine all the ingredients for the filling and spread evenly over the dough. Cut the dough into six long strips and roll up the first one. Place the roll on the second strip and roll up. Continue until all the dough is used up. Place in a buttered 8 in (20 cm) spring release tin, cover with oiled polythene and leave in a warm place to rise for about 1 hour or until doubled in size.

Bake at 375°F/190°C/gas mark 5 for 45–50 minutes. Brush with honey and leave to cool in the tin.

Makes 1 loaf

SELKIRK BANNOCK

A heavily fruited Scottish teacake.

Sultanas 6–8 oz (175–225 g)
Wholemeal flour 8 oz (225 g)
Salt ½ tsp (2.5 ml)
Butter 1½ oz (40 g)
Unrefined brown sugar 1½ oz (40 g)
Milk ¼ pt (150 ml)
Fresh yeast ½ oz (15 g)
Beaten egg to glaze

Just cover the sultanas with boiling water and leave on one side.

Mix the flour and salt together and rub in the butter.

Place the sugar and milk in a saucepan and warm gently until tepid. Remove from the heat and stir in the yeast. Add the yeast liquid to the dry mixture and mix well.

Drain the sultanas, dry them thoroughly on a kitchen cloth and add to the dough. Mix well, cover and leave in a warm place for 45 minutes.

Knead the dough on a lightly-floured surface and shape into a neat round. Place on an oiled baking tray and flatten to an 8 in (20 cm) round. Cover with oiled polythene and leave to rise in a warm place for about 45 minutes, until doubled in size.

Brush with beaten egg and bake at 425°F/220°C/ gas mark 7 for about 25 minutes. Cool on a wire tray.

Makes 1 loaf

FRUIT BREAD

If you can resist this loaf long enough for it to go stale, it's wonderful toasted and spread with butter!

Fresh yeast 1 oz (25 g)
Molasses 2 oz (50 g)
Water, tepid 8 fl oz (250 ml)
Wholemeal flour 1 lb (450 g)
Salt 1 tsp (5 ml)
Ground cinnamon ½ tsp (2.5 ml)
Ground mixed spice ½ tsp (2.5 ml)
Ground ginger ½ tsp (2.5 ml)
Ground allspice ¼ tsp (1.25 ml)
Ground nutmeg ¼ tsp (1.25 ml)
Free-range egg, beaten 1
Raisins 2 oz (50 g)
Currants 2 oz (50 g)
Sultanas 2 oz (50 g)
Walnuts, chopped 2 oz (50 g)
Oil to glaze
Apple concentrate to glaze

Mix the yeast, molasses and water and leave in a warm place for about 10 minutes until frothy.

Combine the flour, salt and spices in a large bowl. Add the beaten egg and yeast liquid and mix to a soft dough. Knead for 7–8 minutes on a lightly-floured surface. Work in the fruit and walnuts.

Divide the dough in half, knead each portion quickly then transfer to two oiled 1 lb (450 g) loaf tins. Brush lightly with oil. Cover with oiled polythene and leave in a warm place until doubled in size – about 45 minutes.

Bake at 400°F/200°C/gas mark 6 for 25–30 minutes. Cool on a wire tray. Brush the surface of each loaf with apple concentrate, while still warm.

Makes 2 loaves

YORKSHIRE TEACAKES

Fresh yeast 1 oz (25 g)
Unrefined brown sugar 1 oz & 1 tsp (25 g & 5 ml)
Milk, tepid ½ pt (300 ml)
Wholemeal flour 1 lb (450 g)
Salt 1 tsp (5 ml)
Butter or nutter 1 oz (25 g)
Currants 2 oz (50 g)
Sugar glaze (see p. 92)

Mix the yeast, 1 tsp (5 ml) of the sugar and the milk together and leave in a warm place until frothy – about 10 minutes.

Combine the flour and salt in a large bowl. Rub in the butter and stir in the remaining sugar. Add the yeast liquid and mix to a soft dough.

Knead for 7–8 minutes, then work in the currants.

Divide the dough into six portions. On a lightly-floured surface, knead each portion into a round. Place well apart on buttered baking trays. Cover with oiled polythene and leave in a warm place until doubled in size – 30–40 minutes.

Brush with sugar glaze and bake at 425°F/220°C/gas mark 7 for 15–20 minutes. Cool on a wire tray.

Makes 6

APPLE & BANANA BREAD

An unusual combination of fruit which permeates
through the loaf.

Medium cooking apple, cored 1
Wholemeal flour 1 lb (450 g)
Fresh yeast ½ oz (15 g)
Water, tepid ¼ pt (150 ml)
Unrefined brown sugar 2 oz (50 g)
Salt 1 tsp (5 ml)
Ground cinnamon 1 tsp (5 ml)
Ground nutmeg 1 tsp (5 ml)
Sultanas 2 oz (50 g)
Small bananas, mashed 2
Lemon, finely grated rind of ½
Apple concentrate to glaze

Chop and steam the apple until tender and press
through a sieve to make a purée. Leave to cool.

Mix together 4 oz (100 g) flour, the yeast and water
and leave in a warm place until frothy – about 10
minutes.

Combine the remaining flour, sugar, salt, spices and
sultanas in a large bowl. Stir in the yeast mixture,
apple purée, mashed banana and lemon rind and
knead for 5 minutes. Place on a lightly-floured surface
and divide into two portions. Shape and place into
two oiled 1 lb (450 g) loaf tins. Cover with oiled
polythene and leave in a warm place until doubled in
size – about 1 hour.

Bake at 400°F/200°C/gas mark 6 for 35 minutes.
Remove from the oven and glaze with the apple
concentrate. Cool on a wire tray.

Makes 2 loaves

QUICK PRUNE BREAD

Wholemeal flour 8 oz (225 g)
Unrefined brown sugar 4 oz (100 g)
Bicarbonate of soda ½ tsp (2.5 ml)
Baking powder ¼ tsp (1.25 ml)
Salt ¼ tsp (1.25 ml)
Prunes – ready to eat, pitted and chopped 4 oz (100 g)
Oil 1 tbsp (15 ml)
Free-range egg, beaten 1
Unsweetened prune juice 2 tbsp (30 ml)
Buttermilk 4 fl oz (100 ml)

Mix all the dry ingredients together in a bowl. Stir in the oil, egg, prune juice and buttermilk quickly and transfer to a buttered and base-lined 1 lb (450 g) loaf tin.

Bake at 350°F/180°C/gas mark 4 for about 1 hour until risen and firm to the touch. Cool on a wire tray.

Makes 1 loaf

GYPSY MALT LOAF

This loaf becomes more moist with keeping.

Wholemeal flour 8 oz (225 g)
Salt, a pinch
Bicarbonate of soda 1 tsp (5 ml)
Raisins 2 oz (50 g)
Sultanas 2 oz (50 g)
Dried dates, chopped 2 oz (50 g)
Black treacle 2 oz (50 g)
Malt extract 2 oz (50 g)
Unrefined brown sugar 1 oz (25 g)
Milk ¼ pt (150 ml)

Mix the flour, salt and bicarbonate of soda in a bowl. Stir in the fruits. Warm the treacle, malt extract and sugar together until the sugar is dissolved. Add to the dry ingredients with the milk. Mix quickly until evenly combined, then transfer to a buttered and base-lined 1 lb (450 g) loaf tin.

Level the surface and bake at 350°F/180°C/gas mark 4 for about 1 hour until risen and firm to the touch. Cool on a wire tray.

Wrap and store for at least three days before eating. Serve in slices with butter.

Makes 1 loaf

SUGAR-CRUSTED WALNUT
TEABREAD

Fresh yeast ½ oz (15 g)
Unrefined brown sugar 2 tsp (10 ml)
Water, tepid ⅓ pt (200 ml)
Wholemeal flour 10 oz (300 g)
Rolled oats 2 oz (50 g)
Wheatgerm ½ oz (15 g)
Salt 1 tsp (5 ml)
Honey 2 tbsp (30 ml)
Walnut oil 2 tbsp (30 ml)
Egg glaze (see p. 92)
Unrefined demerara sugar 2 tbsp (30 ml)

Mix together the yeast, sugar and water, and leave in a
warm place until frothy – about 10 minutes. Combine
the flour, oats, wheatgerm and salt in a bowl.

Add the yeast liquid to the flour mixture, together
with the honey and walnut oil. Mix to a soft dough.
Knead for 8–10 minutes, then transfer to a lightly-
floured surface. Knead quickly and place in a lightly-
oiled 1 lb (450 g) loaf tin. Cover with oiled polythene
and leave in a warm place until doubled in size –
about 35–40 minutes.

Brush with egg glaze and sprinkle with the sugar.
Bake at 400°F/200°C/gas mark 6 for 35 minutes. Cool
on a wire tray.

Makes 1 loaf

PEAR, GINGER & SULTANA BRAID

A delicious fruit filling encased in a plait of enriched
bread.

FILLING
Sultanas 8 oz (225 g)
Orange juice 4 fl oz (100 ml)
Pears, cored and chopped 1 lb (450 g)
Orange, finely grated rind of 1
Unrefined brown sugar 1 oz (25 g)
Crystallized ginger, chopped 2 oz (50 g)

DOUGH
Fresh yeast ¾ oz (20 g)
Water, tepid 6 fl oz (175 ml)
Unrefined brown sugar 1 oz (25 g)
Wholemeal flour 14 oz (400 g)
Salt 1 tsp (5 ml)
Skimmed milk powder 2 tbsp (30 ml)
Butter 1 oz (25 g)
Free-range egg, beaten 1
Egg glaze (see p. 92)
Pear concentrate to glaze

For the filling, place the sultanas and orange juice in a
saucepan and simmer for 5 minutes. Add the
remaining ingredients and cook over medium heat,
stirring frequently for a further 10 minutes, or until
there is no free liquid. Leave to cool.

For the dough, mix the yeast, water and sugar and
leave in a warm place for about 10 minutes until
frothy.

Combine the flour, salt and milk powder in a large
bowl. Rub in the butter. Add the beaten egg and yeast
liquid and mix to a soft dough. Knead for 8–10
minutes. Then roll out on a lightly-floured surface to

an oblong about 16×12 in (40×30 cm) and spoon the filling down the centre along its length.

Make 1 in (2.5 cm) cuts from the filling to the outside edge on both sides, then fold the strips in alternately to give a braided effect.

Place on a buttered baking tray and brush with egg glaze.

Cover and leave in a warm place for 15–30 minutes until slightly risen.

Bake at 400°F/200°C/gas mark 6 for 30 minutes until golden. Cool on a wire tray and brush with pear concentrate. Serve warm.

Makes 1 loaf

PLUM PIZZA STREUSEL

A bread crust topped with fresh plums and a crispy coconut layer.

Fresh yeast ¾ oz (20 g)
Unrefined brown sugar 2 oz (50 g)
Water, tepid 8 fl oz (250 ml)
Wholemeal flour 14 oz (400 g)
Salt 1 tsp (5 ml)
Butter 1 oz (25 g)

TOPPING
Plums, stoned and quartered 1½ lb (675 g)
Unrefined light brown sugar 4 oz (100 g)
Wholemeal flour 2 oz (50 g)
Desiccated coconut 2 oz (50 g)
Butter, melted 3 oz (75 g)

Mix the yeast, with a teaspoonful (5 ml) of the sugar

and the water. Leave in a warm place until frothy –
about 10 minutes.

Mix the flour, remaining sugar and salt in a large
bowl. Rub in the butter. Add the yeast liquid and mix
to a soft dough.

Knead for 8–10 minutes. On a lightly-floured
surface, roll out the dough to an oblong and press
neatly and evenly into a buttered Swiss roll tin
13×9 in (33×23 cm).

Prick the surface with a fork. Arrange the quartered
plums on top.

Combine the remaining ingredients for the topping
and sprinkle over the plums. Cover and leave to rise
in a warm place for 30 minutes.

Bake at 375°F/190°C/gas mark 5 for 30–40 minutes.

Cool slightly in the tin then cut into squares. Serve
warm.

Makes 12 squares

FESTIVE STOLLEN

A delicious variation of this Austrian sweet bread.

Rum or orange juice 4 fl oz (100 ml)
Raisins 5 oz (150 g)
Dried papaya pieces 3 oz (75 g)
Fresh yeast 1 oz (25 g)
Unrefined brown sugar 1 tbsp (15 ml)
Milk, tepid 4 fl oz (100 ml)
Wholemeal flour 1 lb (450 g)
Salt 1 tsp (5 ml)
Free-range eggs, beaten 2
Butter, melted 3 oz (75 g)

Lemon, finely grated rind of 1
Pistachio nuts 2 oz (50 g)
Almonds, chopped 2 oz (50 g)
Butter, melted to glaze

Place the rum, raisins and papaya in a bowl. Cover and leave for up to 24 hours to marinate.

Mix the yeast, sugar and milk and leave in a warm place until frothy – about 10 minutes.

Combine the flour and salt, add the yeast liquid, eggs, butter, lemon rind and any juice from the soaked raisins and papaya. Mix to a soft dough and knead for 5–7 minutes. Add the soaked fruits and nuts and knead again for 3 minutes, adding a little tepid water if necessary to give a soft, smooth dough.

On a lightly-floured surface, roll out the dough to an oval about 11 in (28 cm) long and 9 in (23 cm) wide. Fold one-third of the dough over partly to cover the other two-thirds to make the traditional stollen shape.

Place on an oiled baking tray, cover with oiled polythene and leave in a warm place to rise until doubled in size – 2–3 hours.

Bake at 375°F/190°C/gas mark 5 for 45 minutes. Brush with melted butter and cool on a wire tray. If wished, tie a ribbon around the centre of the stollen.

Variation
Roll 8 oz (225 g) marzipan into an 11 in (28 cm) length. Place on the prepared dough before folding. Continue as above.

Makes 1 loaf

HOT CROSS BUNS

Cranks bakes thousands of these delicious spicy buns
every Easter.

Fresh yeast 1 oz (25 g)
Milk, tepid 8 fl oz (250 ml)
Unrefined brown sugar 4 oz (100 g)
Wholemeal flour 8 oz (225 g)
Barley flour 8 oz (225 g)
Salt 1 tsp (5 ml)
Butter 2 oz (50 g)
Ground mixed spice 1 tsp (5 ml)
Ground cinnamon ¾ tsp (3.75 ml)
Ground allspice ½ tsp (2.5 ml)
Ground nutmeg ¼ tsp (1.25 ml)
Free-range egg, beaten 1
Currants 4 oz (100 g)

PASTE
85% wholemeal flour 1 oz (25 g)
Water 2 tbsp (30 ml)

GLAZE
Clear honey 1 tbsp (15 ml)
Apple concentrate 1 tbsp (15 ml)

Mix the yeast, milk and 2 tsp (10 ml) of the sugar and
leave in a warm place until frothy – about 10 minutes.

Combine the flours with the salt. Rub in the butter.
Add the remaining sugar, spices, egg and yeast liquid.
Knead for 5 minutes, then work in the currants.

Place the dough on a lightly-floured surface. Divide
into 12 portions. Shape each portion into a round.

Place the 12 rounds on a lightly oiled 13×9 in
(33×23 cm) Swiss roll tin. Cover with oiled polythene
and leave in a warm place until doubled in size –
about 2 hours.

For the paste, mix the flour with the water. Make a small greaseproof paper piping bag or snip the corner off a small strong polythene bag and fill with the paste. Pipe a cross over each bun. Bake at 400°F/200°C/gas mark 6 for about 25 minutes. Mix the honey with the apple concentrate and glaze the buns. Cool on a wire tray.

Makes 12

SPICY BUCKWHEAT BUNS

These unusual buns are made from three gluten-free flours. Best served warm.

Milk ½ pt (300 ml)
Lemon juice 1 tbsp (15 ml)
Buckwheat flour 5 oz (150 g)
Brown rice flour 5 oz (150 g)
Potato flour 5 oz (150 g)
Butter 2 oz (50 g)
Unrefined brown sugar 2 oz (50 g)
Ground cinnamon 1 tsp (5 ml)
Ground mixed spice 2 tsp (10 ml)
Bicarbonate of soda 1½ tsp (7.5 ml)
Cream of tartar 1 tbsp (15 ml)
Currants 2 oz (50 g)
Sultanas 2 oz (50 g)

Mix the milk with the lemon juice. Combine the flours and rub in the butter. Add the remaining ingredients and mix thoroughly to a soft dough. With floured hands shape the dough into 14 balls. Place the balls on a lightly-oiled baking tray and flatten slightly. Bake at 400°F/200°C/gas mark 6 for 20–25 minutes. Cool on a wire tray.

Makes 14

BATH BUNS

Made in the Cranks way!

Fresh yeast ¾ oz (20 g)
Milk, tepid ¼ pt (150 ml)
Unrefined brown sugar 2 oz (50 g)
Wholemeal flour 12 oz (350 g)
Salt, a pinch
Free-range egg, beaten 1
Lemon, finely grated rind of 1
Sultanas 4 oz (100 g)
Butter, softened 4 oz (100 g)
Beaten egg to glaze
Unrefined cane sugar cubes, roughly crushed to sprinkle

Mix the yeast with the milk, a teaspoon (5 ml) of the sugar and 2 tablespoons (30 mls) of the flour until smooth. Leave in a warm place for about 10 minutes until frothy.

Mix the remaining flour and sugar together in a bowl. Add the salt, the yeast mixture, egg, lemon rind and sultanas. Mix to a smooth dough, then work in the butter until smooth once more.

Cover and leave in a warm place for 30 minutes.

Knead the dough on a lightly-floured surface, then divide the mixture into 12 even portions. Shape each one into a ball. Place on buttered baking trays, cover and leave in a warm place until doubled in size – 30–45 minutes.

Brush with beaten egg and sprinkle with the crushed sugar. Bake at 425°F/220°C/gas mark 7 for about 15 minutes until risen and golden brown. Cool on a wire tray.

Makes 12

EGG GLAZE

Free-range egg 1
Milk 3 tbsp (45 ml)

Beat the egg and milk together until evenly combined.

SUGAR GLAZE

Unrefined brown sugar 1 oz (25 g)
Water 8 fl oz (250 ml)

Dissolve the sugar in the water in a saucepan over
gentle heat. Leave to cool.

SALT GLAZE

Salt 2 tsp (10 ml)
Water 2 tbsp (30 ml)

Dissolve the salt in the water in a saucepan over
gentle heat. Leave to cool.

INDEX